Plant Management
Essential Leadership in Manufacturing Facilities

Louis Bevoc, Rachael Collinson, and Allison Shearsett

Published by
Nutriniche System LLC

For information contact:
info@nutriniche.com

I0491541

Louis Bevoc books...simple explanations of complex subjects

Risk management

Audits

Social responsibility

Summary

Introduction

Manufacturing facilities, sometimes called factories or production plants, are industrial sites where people and machinery are used to create items that are sold to customers. These facilities often employ people on assembly lines where a product moves from one station to the next with each station adding a different component until the product is finished. The assembly concept was developed during the industrial revolution and it is still considered the fastest and most cost-effective method for people to mass-create items...especially when compared to the old way of having individuals assemble entire products by themselves.

Plant managers are often the most important employees in manufacturing facilities. They are in charge of all aspects of plant operations, and they interact with virtually everyone involved with the business....from suppliers to customers. This involvement makes it understandable why their jobs can become 24 hours per day, 7 days per week if they do not possess the necessary management, interpersonal, and organizational skills to fulfill their job requirements while maintaining the support of their subordinates and coworkers.

Plant managers are involved with present and long-term plans for their facilities. In addition to overseeing production, they are responsible for maintenance, engineering, safety, quality, warehousing, inventory control, and building projects. They monitor costs and expenditures and bear responsibility for all plant-related projects, processes, policies, and procedures. Since they deal with people at all levels, plant management professionals are very visible and always in demand.

This book examines the unique individuals who assume roles as plant managers. It analyzes what they do and how they function while describing the problems they must overcome to perform at peak levels. It also shows how challenging it can be to become an effective plant manager by highlighting the many different skills that these leaders must possess. Seven major areas of discussion include manufacturing, management, human resource management, organizational development, risk management, audits, and social responsibility. The material is written for easy reader understanding at all levels and is an excellent source for beginners or those seeking general knowledge about the subject matter.

Now that you understand the scope of this book, let's move into the first section which details plant management responsibilities in manufacturing.

Manufacturing

Manufacturing is all of the activities that take place while a product is being made. It starts with the receiving of raw materials and ends with finished products being shipped out of the building. Below are the departments that are a part of manufacturing along with the roles and responsibilities of plant managers overseeing the function of those departments.

Production

Production is the process of assembling, combining, or putting together various raw materials to create finished products. These finished products have value to the customers who purchase them because they can be sold as they are or used to build other items. For example, a tool manufacturer sells bolts to a hardware store that resells them to the public. However, the tool manufacturer also sells the same bolts to a company that uses them in the manufacturing of snowmobile engines. In both cases, the bolts have value, but one company sees the value in its original form while the other sees it as being useful for making something else.

Production is the heart of a manufacturing plant. Without it, products do not get made and cannot be sold. If there are no sales, then there is no money to pay for people and supplies. Since most people are opposed to working for free, it is only a matter of time before the plant ceases operations.

Production is based upon productivity, and, as mentioned in the introduction, productivity in a manufacturing plant is typically best when assembly line operations are employed. Plant managers make sure productivity is meeting pre-determined requirements by working with production supervisors. These supervisors oversee specific areas of the production process and provide information to the plant manager that shows whether or not expectations are being met. If production personnel are not meeting expectations, then the plant manager must implement changes to correct the problems.

Production management can be quite challenging because one size does not fit all. For example, a razor blade manufacturing plant might make more than fifty percent of its razors with two blades. However, there is also a demand for one-blade, three-blade, four-blade, and five-blade razors. Each blade type requires a different set-up and assembly process so proper scheduling is necessary to assure the most efficient process and least number of change-overs. Plant managers usually do not do the scheduling themselves, but they oversee that being done by their production supervisors to assure it is correct.

Plant managers also oversee all of the costs associated with production. They monitor employee labor, product yields, and production overhead costs to assure that they are adhering to established standards. If those standards are not being met, then plant managers must make changes to bring the production activities back into compliance.

In high-volume, high-speed plants, production costs are often the most important aspect of plant managers' jobs. In fact, their job status sometimes depends on keeping those costs below certain thresholds. It is not unusual for plant managers to receive bonuses one year based on low costs and then be threatened with losing their jobs the next year when those costs increase. This might seem rather harsh, but it is a reality in the world of plant management.

Quality

It is difficult, if not impossible, for companies to gain market share without some type of quality program in place. These programs must be understood and taken seriously by all personnel or they will fail to achieve goals and be effective. They require implementation and monitoring by skilled individuals who embrace change and are able to work in challenging environments. These individuals are known as quality assurance and quality control employees, and they work in quality departments of organizations.

Although they work toward the same goals and objectives, there is a difference between quality assurance and quality control employees. Quality assurance personnel make sure quality procedures are appropriate and in place for products. They assure the quality of products by establishing standards that prevent defects. For example, a soap manufacturing plant needs to make sure black cherry soap meets a color requirement. The quality assurance people develop a color chart that can be used as a standard. This chart is implemented in the plant as a mandatory color check on every batch of soap before packaging.

Quality assurance personnel control the quality of products using established standards that detect defects. Consider the black cherry soap example in the soap manufacturing plant. Quality control technicians use the color chart developed by quality assurance people to check every batch of product before packaging. If the color does not match, the soap is rejected.

Continuous improvement is the main goal of quality departments because it employs the thinking that everything can be better. There is no status quo, and efforts are constantly made to raise the bar. Some of the changes resulting from this process are immediately apparent, while others are not so obvious and take time to transpire. Changes that transpire over time are often the preferred method of continuous improvement because they allow employees time to adjust to workplace modifications.

In manufacturing plants, quality personnel are required to work toward continuous improvement. They develop procedures that improve processes and assure products adhere to specified quality standards. This allows their companies to sell consistent products and remain competitive in markets that demand uniformity. However, as might be expected, there are challenges involved with maintaining high-quality standards...especially if those standards are in direct contrast with production goals. Production people have jobs to do, and they sometimes object to their jobs being hindered by quality requirements even if those requirements prevent future problems. When conflicts of this nature arise, plant managers must step in and resolve them. They need to make decisions that back quality actions regardless of whether or not production suffers. This can be difficult, but it is a necessary job requirement for those in plant management roles.

Below are some of the major job responsibilities of quality personnel in manufacturing plants.

Conformance

Conformance is the process of getting goods and services to adhere to predetermined criteria. In manufacturing, conformance is the degree to which products meet established standards commonly known as benchmarks. Benchmarks can be standards that need to be met on every production run, such as a box company achieving the same thickness on every corrugated carton, or they can raise the bar with the ultimate goal of continuous improvement, such as a computer manufacturer striving to continually lower defects.

The responsibility for conforming to benchmarks typically falls on the shoulders of quality personnel. They monitor and enforce conformance of products using two somewhat different standards as follows:

Internal standards

Internal standards are those established for the organization, and they are not necessarily the same as external (regulatory or customer) standards. Many times these standards are put in place for cost or yield purposes. For example, a saw manufacturing company might have a customer requirement (external standard) that blades must have a minimum thickness of .1 inches. However, quality personnel also make sure the blades adhere to an internal standard that prohibits the maximum thickness from exceeding .13 inches. In this instance, quality employees are making sure the saw manufacturer does not "give away" the metal used to make the blades so the company's costs remain in line with the selling price.

External standards

External standards are those established based on regulatory and/or customer requirements. For example, a beverage manufacturer might have a government requirement (external standard) that designates s a plastic bottle must contain at least

2.0 liters of a beverage. In contrast, an internal standard for this bottle might be that it can contain no more than 2.05 liters of beverage to avoid "give away" and maintain product yields for costing purposes. The government requires a minimum beverage volume standard that must be adhered to by the manufacturer, but the government does not specify a maximum volume standard even though it is enforced by quality personnel via an internal standard.

Regardless of the type of standard, conformance is important in manufacturing because it regulates the products being manufactured. Quality personnel are hired to uphold established standards, and conformance ranks as one of their top job responsibilities.

Consistency

Consistency is similar to conformance, but it refers to making the same product every time rather than meeting standards. For example, assume a chemical manufacturer produces a toilet bowl cleaner that contains bleach. A retail store chain buying this product establishes an external requirement that this product must contain at least five percent bleach. The chemical manufacturer implements an internal standard of no more than five and one-half percent bleach in the toilet bowl cleaner. However, to be consistent, the product formulation designates 5.1 percent bleach in every batch. This standard assures that customers will be satisfied and the company will make money, so consistency needs to be monitored by quality personnel.

Another reason for consistency is public perception of the organization. The chemical manufacturer does not want the reputation of being "consistently inconsistent," so they hire quality personnel to watch every batch to assure the amount of bleach added is always the same. Consistent products lead to repeat customers because they continually come back to purchase items that they know will perform the same every time they are used.

Unfortunately, consistency is one of the most overlooked aspects of manufacturing, and it is a major reason why quality personnel are in place. Companies want to make the same product time after time, but a wide variety of factors contribute to this not happening. These factors include:

Raw material changes

Raw material can change when manufacturers change suppliers because these new suppliers might not sell the exact same products. An example is a door manufacturing company that decides to buy handles from a new supplier. These handles might not be the same type, design, or composition; thereby jeopardizing the quality of the finished door.

New suppliers are not the only threat to consistency in terms of raw material changes.

Current suppliers also present challenges when they decide to make changes regarding their materials, processes, or procedures. For example, a supplier of molds might decide to change their metal to a lower grade of steel; thereby affecting the consistency of the manufacturer's finished product.

Current suppliers also threaten consistency when they short raw materials orders because they force manufacturers to make changes to their formulations or processes. For example, a meat plant might add three percent soy protein to a sausage product, but when their supplier does not completely fill their order, they need to reduce the soy protein added to two percent; thereby affecting the consistency of the finished sausage.

Formulation changes

This refers to formulation changes made by the manufacturer. Formulas are changed for a variety of reasons reduced raw material costs, time savings, improved quality, and better product yields. For example, a bakery might decide to use artificial vanilla instead of the more expensive vanilla extract, so their consistency changes due to lower raw material costs.

The bakery might also decide to save time on their bread manufacturing line by shortening the mixing process. They realize that they can make more bread every shift if they reduce the mixing time of each batch. This increases productivity-related aspects of the plant, but it also impacts consistency of the finished loaves of bread.

Regardless of the reason, formulation changes alter product consistency. Customers who do not like these changes react by purchasing similar products from competitors resulting in sales problems for the manufacturer.

Processing changes

Manufacturers can change their processes voluntarily or involuntarily. For example, some managers deliberately change machinery, equipment, or personnel for cost reduction purposes. Their actions are calculated and planned meaning changes in consistency result from intentional decisions.

However, not all actions related to process changes are voluntary. Some changes are forced on manufacturers for reasons beyond their control. Machines become obsolete or parts are no longer able to be ordered, so changes need to be made. The decisions to change are brought about by uncontrollable circumstances, and they affect product consistency.

Regardless of the initial catalyst, processing changes impact product consistency....and the resulting customer complaints cause headaches for manufacturers.

One last important point about consistency is that consistent products are not always good. If a company manufactures a consistently bad product, then consistency has a negative impact on consumer perception. Quality personnel need to understand that this can happen, and their job is to react by suggesting ideas for improvement.

Calibration

Quality personnel are charged with the responsibility of calibrating many different types of equipment in manufacturing facilities. This equipment is found in laboratories, pilot plants, production areas, and even offices. It includes analyzers, meters, scales, thermometers, and other equipment that is needed for manufacturing processes.

Calibration is an important aspect of manufacturing because it makes sure devices used for measuring or analyzing are accurate. The keyword is "accurate" because inaccurate measurement creates problems for manufacturers. For example, a scale that is wrongly calibrated will give a false weight every time it is used. If it is a scale used to weight finished products for retail stores, then the customer is never receiving the amount on the package. This problem is compounded for underweight products because the government can issue fines.

Safety is another reason for calibration because inaccurate measurements can injure consumers or make them sick. For example, an uncalibrated food thermometer used to take the temperatures of hot dogs in a meat plant could give a reading higher than the actual temperature; thereby causing consumers who purchase the product to get sick from foodborne illness.

One last reason that calibration is needed is certification. Certification is support that products and services meet specific criteria or fall within designated tolerances. For example, a certified paint testing laboratory can assure an elementary school that the paint used in the building is lead-free. The laboratory's testing procedure is certified by an official governing body, assuring the school administrators and parents of the children that it is accurate.

In short, calibration prevents errors that can occur in manufacturing facilities. Quality personnel are well aware of the consequences of those errors, and that is a major reason why they are charged with implementing and upholding calibration processes and procedures.

Analysis

Analysis is used in manufacturing to examine something in detail to make an interpretation or determination. Often this involves breaking down or separating individual components for a better understanding. For example, hay is analyzed for moisture to determine if it is ready to sell without the risk of mold or bacterial issues. This analysis involves separating water from the other hay components to determine the moisture content for decision-making purposes.

In terms of job responsibilities, calibration often goes hand-in-hand with analysis for quality personnel. First, they calibrate devices to make sure they are accurate and in proper working order. Then they use the calibrated devices to perform analyses...usually in laboratory settings. For example, a quality person at a dairy calibrates a fat analyzer and then uses it to determine the amount of fat in skim milk.

Statistical process control (SPC) is a specific type of analysis. Essentially, SPC is a form of quality control that collects, interprets, and analyzes data to see if it meets specifications. This type of analysis is employed by quality personnel in a wide variety of manufacturing organizations for problem prevention and continuous improvement.

Analysis is an expected job responsibility of quality personnel in most manufacturing facilities. They need to analyze various aspects of production to assure that products and processes are performing as anticipated.

Quality is a major concern of plant managers in charge of most manufacturing companies. They want people to perceive their businesses as high-end operations that care about their products and services and the customers who purchase them. They believe that the cost of quality is a fraction of the payback, and their organizations' will be the beneficiaries. In the end, defects go down as profitability increases...and this makes stakeholders happy.

Safety

Safety is quite possibly the most important concern of plant management in manufacturing environments. When someone gets seriously injured or killed, no amount of money or other compensation can make up for the pain and suffering. A permanent scare is left that never goes away, and the people in charge of the plant are held responsible

Safety should be a major concern of everyone in a manufacturing plant, but, unfortunately, unsafe practices take place and that is why safety rules, regulations, and departments are necessary. Plant managers oversee safety departments, so they need to have a good understanding of what those departments need to do to keep the workforce safe. This understanding is quite complex and includes the issues listed below.

Machinery

Manufacturing plants need machines because they enable companies to produce far more products than they could ever make using human labor alone. For this reason, machinery in manufacturing facilities will always be present in the environment.

Unfortunately, the downside to machinery is the constant threat of operator injury...or even death in extreme cases. Machines have chains, pulleys, sprockets, and other moving parts that pose safety threats to the operators and employees in the immediate vicinity. One example is a finger, hand, or entire limb being severed by s sharp edge. Another example is hair becoming caught in rotating parts causing scalping or entanglement. A third example is an air hose breaking off resulting in an employee losing an eye. A complete list of potential harm to employees is too extensive and graphic for this book, but the point is that machines are very capable of injuring workers. That being said, the following adds to the likelihood that machines will cause harm:

- *Disrepair* - It should not come as a surprise that machines in manufacturing facilities break down over time. They get repetitive use, for up to 24 hours a day, and their demise is ultimately inevitable. What might be surprising is the fact that these machines are often not repaired when they do break down as long...as they continue to function. They are left to deteriorate even further with operators doing their best to keep them running. This type of environment sets the stage for injuries as employees tamper with machine parts that they know little or nothing about. For this reason, the disrepair of machinery is a major safety concern that often times does not receive the attention that it deserves.

- *Age* - Along the same lines of disrepair, the age of machinery also poses a safety hazard. Some machines have been properly maintained, but they are simply too old to function as designed or intended. They become worn out and can no longer be repaired...and this causes safety issues that only get worse with time. Father time is relentless, and machines that become too old pose the potential to harm employees until they are removed or replaced.

- *Temporary fixes* - Most people are well aware that temporary fixes are not the answers to problems because they are not permanent solutions. However, temporary fixes are quite common in manufacturing facilities because they allow employees to keep working. Also known as "Band-Aids," these repairs are sometimes more dangerous than doing nothing at all because employees believe their machines are working properly. Workers go back to their normal mode of operation, only to have the temporary fix break without warning....and they end up getting injured. Temporary fixes can cause major problems in terms of worker safety, but, unfortunately, this is not understood by some leaders of manufacturing facilities.

- *Noise* - Many people find noise to be annoying, but it has the potential to cause far more severe problems in manufacturing facilities. The most obvious issue is that it can damage employees' hearing unless they are wearing some type of ear protection. Over time, hearing damage can become permanent causing workers problems in all aspects of their jobs. However, less obvious safety threats from noise also exist. When workers lose their sense of hearing, they are unaware of the danger that lurks in manufacturing plants. They cannot hear warning signals that indicate safety issues, and this exposes them to safety problems without an opportunity to react appropriately to protect their well-being. Additionally, noise can interfere with verbal communication which increases the chance of accidents due to the inability to hear what others are saying.

- *Lack of preventative maintenance* - Preventative maintenance is critical for manufacturers who want to keep their machines operating effectively and efficiently. Regularly scheduled maintenance prevents machines from failing, and it also protects machine operators. In fact, preventative maintenance is one of the most common reasons that operators get hurt. Machines can injure or kill people in seconds...especially if they are not maintained.

Chemicals

Most manufacturing plants use chemicals in some capacity. The chemicals can be purchased for servicing reasons, such as those used for cleaning equipment, or they can be a necessary part of the machine or its parts, such as the acid found in batteries. Regardless of the method of entry into the facility, these chemicals present safety threats to employees working around them.

The following are major areas in manufacturing facilities where chemical risks are present:

- *Sanitation* - Most manufacturing facilities need to be cleaned, but some need more cleaning than others. For example, pharmaceutical and food plants need to be frequently cleaned. Floors, walls, ceilings, equipment, and machinery must be cleaned and sanitized to prevent any type of contamination.

  The majority of cleaning that takes place in manufacturing plants requires the use of chemicals. These chemicals can be strong caustic or alkaline-based products that have the potential to injure employees who come in contact with them. For this reason, cleaning chemicals are a safety risk for employees.

- *Laboratories* - Anyone who is familiar with chemistry laboratories understands chemicals are needed for the different types of analyses that are performed. Testing requires different strengths of potentially harmful chemicals that are handled daily by laboratory technicians. These technicians are typically educated and trained for their jobs, but accidents can and do happen...and this is why laboratories present a safety concern for the employees working in them.

- *Maintenance* - Similar to laboratory employees, maintenance personnel frequently handle potentially hazardous chemicals. They work with various types of Freon, ammonia, paint, oil, gas, lubricants, and other chemicals to service refrigeration units, boilers, vehicles, and machinery. A well-known example is the gasoline used as fuel for engines. It has the potential to catch on fire or explode if not handled properly, and this makes it a safety threat for maintenance employees.

- *Water* (chemicals in drinking water) - Some manufacturers treat water with chlorine, softeners, or pH altering chemicals to make it more suitable for their needs. If the concentrations of these chemicals become excessive, then employees' health can be at risk. This safety threat is rather minor, but it does exist and warrants mention in this section.

The following also pose threats for manufacturers that house chemicals:

- *Improper labeling* - Chemicals that are not properly labeled pose huge safety threats for employees in manufacturing workplaces because those employees risk injury regardless of the precautions taken. They are not aware of the chemicals they are using...making it virtually impossible to prevent misuse. If misuse occurs, then the well-being of everyone is jeopardized, thereby creating a situation that can have devastating effects.

The potential consequences for wrongly labeled chemicals are very serious, and that is why improper labeling is considered an important safety threat in manufacturing facilities.

- *Improper usage* - Proper labeling of chemicals does not prevent improper usage. All the signage, instructions, warnings, and training are useless if employees choose to use chemicals wrongly. For example, a worker might believe that mixing two chemical cleaners will produce one "super cleaner" that has twice the strength. This might be true, but it can also cause toxic fumes or explosions.

Improper usage also results from inadequate training. Employees are at serious risk if they have not been shown how, when, where, and why they should use chemicals in their facilities. Much can be written about the training and improper usage, and that is discussed in the training section of this book.

Unfortunately, improper usage of chemicals in manufacturing facilities can be intentional. Perpetrators fully understand the damage that chemicals can cause, and they used them to attack others. When this happens, it is considered an act of terrorism that threatens the safety of all employees.

- *Improper storage* - One might question why improper storage of chemicals in manufacturing plants poses safety risks to employees. After all, these chemicals are not being used or handled...so what is the problem? In reality, improperly stored chemicals present a few different types of safety hazards. For example, they can leak and contaminate the ground or surrounding water. This poses a major threat to employees' drinking water, and it also threatens everyone else who drinks from the same water source. Leaks that do not contaminate the ground or water also pose threats if employees come in contact with the chemical. An example is a battery that leaks acid. Employees who touch that acid by mistake can experience chemical burns.

Another issue involving chemical storage involves damage. In busy manufacturing facilities, damage to inventory is inevitable. Chemicals are part of a plant's inventory and they can be damaged by pallet jacks or forklifts. If this happens, the surrounding areas become contaminated. Fire is now a safety risk and, in extreme cases, so are explosions.

Properly stored chemicals are typically not a safety risk for employees, but problems result when they are not stored properly. Management needs to realize the potential for problems here and act accordingly by using responsible chemical storage protocols.

Lockout/Tagout

Lockout/Tagout programs are needed by manufacturers because they assure all energy sources of equipment and/or machinery are locked out during service work or maintenance work; thereby protecting employees from being harmed by accidental activation or release of stored energy. Energy sources typically include the following:

- Electricity
- Gas
- Gravity
- Hydraulic
- Kinetic
- Pneumatic
- Thermal

Lockout/Tagout devices are unique because they are individually numbered and keyed. Many times these devices are assigned to specific employees so no one else can open them once they are locked. They are also red in color so they can be easily identified. For safety reasons, these devices have one purpose...to lockout machines or equipment. They cannot be used for locking anything else (bikes, lockers, etc.).

The following are situations where Lockout/Tagout is required:

- *Equipment cleaning or jam-clearing tasks* - When a machine or piece of equipment is stopped for cleaning, clearing, or adjusting.
- *Equipment Repair* - When a repair is being performed...including machinery and equipment from which a guard or other safety device has been removed.
- *Installation* - When machinery or equipment is being installed.
- *Electrical Repair* - When work other than testing is to be performed on an electrical circuit.

In contrast, the following are situations where Lockout/Tagout is not required:

- *Minor tool changes* - When a stop button is used to control unexpected motion during the change or adjustment and when the start button is both visible and under the employee's immediate control.
- *Routine or repetitive minor servicing* - When activities take place during normal production and the work is performed using alternative protective measures that provide effective employee protection.

- *Cord and plug connected equipment* - When the equipment or machine is unplugged and under the exclusive control of the employee performing the service or maintenance.
- *Repair, troubleshooting, and set-up adjustments* - When work on energized equipment or machinery must be done with the machine energized.

Lockout/Tagout programs have prevented injuries and saved lives in many instances. Based on this, manufacturing employees are at risk if Lockout/Tagout devices are not in place as required by OSHA law. Unfortunately, many manufacturers have good Lockout/Tagout programs written, but they are generally disregarded and not taken seriously by the workforce. This problem results from management inefficiency, and it will not correct itself without intervention from those in higher positions. That being said, the biggest safety issue concerning Lockout/Tagout programs is not designing or writing them; it is the failure to implement, maintain, and enforce them...and that is why they are a major safety concern in manufacturing facilities.

Confined spaces

Confined spaces are a reality in manufacturing plants that cannot be avoided. They pose a safety risk list for employees because limited air and escape routes create potentially deadly situations for workers trapped inside them. Unfortunately, some employees do not realize or acknowledge the danger involved even though their lives could be on the line in emergencies.

Confined spaces are sometimes confused with small spaces. The size of the area does not necessarily make a space confined. For a space to be considered confined, it must meet the following criteria:

- It must be large enough for a person to fit into and perform work.
- It must have restricted entry and exit points.
- It must not be designed for continuous occupancy.
- It must have the potential for injury due to the enclosure.

Based on the above criteria, confined spaces in manufacturing facilities include tanks, silos, containers, chambers, bins, pits, crawl spaces, and ceiling gaps. All of these spaces are necessary for manufacturing, and they create situations where injury is possible. Atmospheric issues including fumes, gas, dust, smoke, and lack of oxygen all pose safety issues. For example, flour storage silos in bakeries pose safety risks because combustible dust is very explosive when suspended in the air. Along the same lines, employees working in septic tanks or sewers are exposed to a hazardous gas called methane that carries a risk of exploding... so it is not safe to perform tasks such as welding. Methane also displaces oxygen and makes it difficult to breathe.

Oxygen is an interesting concept in confined spaces because too much or too little can create a safety hazard. Too little oxygen is a result of it being displaced by another gas causing people to experience breathing problems. They can pass out and experience brain damage or death without emergency treatment. Excessive oxygen increases the risk of fire or explosion because some materials spontaneously burn in enriched oxygen conditions.

Flooding is also a threat in confined spaces. For example, water can enter causing people to drown. Unfortunately, water might be the best-case scenario in terms of flooding. Chemical floods can cause skin burns and suffocation....two very unpleasant effects for the workers who experience them.

Maintenance and sanitation workers typically experience the most safety risks in confined spaces because they need to perform some of their job functions in these areas. For example, a maintenance worker might need to go down into a sewer to repair a broken drain. Along the same lines, a sanitation worker might need to be lowered into a flour silo to properly clean it.

The worst part about confined spaces is the fact that many times employees do not realize the danger when entering them. They do not take any precautions and unknowingly proceed as if everything is normal. In a relatively short period of time, they find themselves in an unsafe situation...with the potential to be life-threatening.

Based on the above concerns, it is understandable that plant managers have their hands full in terms of safety in their facilities. That is why they need to have the right people who run and work in their safety departments. Without these individuals, their jobs are much more difficult

Maintenance

Maintenance in manufacturing plants was touched upon in the safety section, but it warrants a section of its own. Three major types of maintenance programs in manufacturing facilities are known as preventative, predictive, and preventative maintenance.

Preventative maintenance

In general, preventative maintenance programs are implemented so future problems can be avoided. For example, tires on a car should be rotated every 8000 miles. This prevents the tires from wearing unevenly and needing to be replaced before the 40,000-mile life expectancy. In a manufacturing facility, preventative maintenance is also designed to prevent future problems from occurring. For example, working machine parts need to be greased weekly to avoid excessive friction that leads to damage.

Like most other aspects of business, preventative maintenance has benefits and drawbacks in manufacturing plants. These positives and negatives must be taken into consideration when deciding whether or not to implement a preventative maintenance program. The time, effort, and money invested in this type of program need to have a payback to be justified...and that justification can only be determined by plant management personnel.

Below are some advantages of preventative maintenance programs.

Risk reduction

Preventative maintenance reduces the risk that there will be failures during production. It provides insurance that production quotas will not be interfered with by broken machinery or faulty equipment. This eliminates a major headache for management personnel and allows them to focus on other areas of their jobs.

Life expectancy

Every manufacturer wants machinery and equipment to last as long as possible in their facilities. This eliminates replacement costs that can be quite significant...especially when machines are designed for a single purpose. That being said, machinery and equipment are expected to last longer when a preventative strategy is utilized because periodic servicing helps maintain them in proper working order. In terms of life expectance, an ounce of prevention is truly worth a pound of cure.

Cost savings

When done properly, preventative maintenance easily justifies its existence economically. It helps (1) prevent maintenance personnel from fixing machines at a later date, (2) avert the need for external sources of repair, (3) avoid unnecessary downtime and the cost of unproductive labor, and (4) eliminate sluggish equipment that slows productivity. Based on these four areas of cost savings, it is rather obvious that the payback for preventative maintenance programs can be substantial.

Energy

This advantage goes largely unnoticed, but it needs to be noted. Machinery and equipment that are not serviced using preventive maintenance are often less energy efficient. They require more electricity or gas to function at desired levels, thereby increasing energy bills and wasting resources. Cost goes down and efficiency goes up when preventative maintenance programs are in place

Below are some disadvantages of preventative maintenance programs.

Immediate costs

There is an up-front cost for preventative maintenance programs. Personnel need to be hired and supplies need to be inventoried. Depending on the number of people hired and the scope of the program, this can be quite expensive...and all of the costs are accrued before the first product leaves the production line. Some companies cannot afford to put out the money, and others simply refuse to do it because they believe the cost is not justified.

Management

This refers to maintenance people and preventative maintenance programs because both of them need to be managed. People require direction, and that direction needs to come from a supervisor. That supervisor also needs to make sure the program is followed and the work required gets done in a timely manner. Management of a preventative maintenance program is not a small task, and that makes it a disadvantage for manufacturers.

Volume changes

When is preventative maintenance too much or too little? This question is difficult to answer, and it can create a problem for manufacturers. For example, a program requires maintenance personnel to replace the wheels on all smokehouse racks in a turkey processing plant every six weeks. This makes sense because racks could break down during production, causing downtime. However, this program does not account for seasonal volume shifts such as Thanksgiving (when production is at a peak), and the summer months (when production is very low). In reality, wheel replacement should be much higher around Thanksgiving and much lower in the summer months...but this is not the case because the preventative maintenance program calls for replacement every six weeks.

Value

Unfortunately, some business leaders believe preventative maintenance is a luxury. As a luxury, it is one of the first areas to undergo cuts when manufacturers are experiencing financial difficulties. From a cost-saving perspective, this makes little sense because the money spent preventing problems is typically less than that spent repairing machinery or equipment that has failed. However, these leaders' thinking will likely never change because preventative maintenance is regarded as a "precautionary" expenditure that is difficult to tie to actual production downtime. If the value of something cannot be directly measured, then number crunchers in the manufacturing organization will push for its elimination during tough times.

Now you understand the advantages and disadvantages of preventative maintenance. This program is beneficial for many manufacturers because it keeps equipment and machinery operating at optimal levels. However, there are some up-front costs involved, and management needs to determine the real value of this program.

Next, let's move into a discussion on a type of program that uses logic and reasoning to assess maintenance needs. That program is known as predictive maintenance.

Predictive maintenance

This is the rarest type of maintenance program used by manufacturers. Essentially, machines and equipment are examined to predict when maintenance should be performed. Similar to preventative maintenance, predictive maintenance is implemented to avoid future problems. However, if done properly, this program costs less than preventative maintenance because service is only performed when justified. In other words, predictions are made about the potential failure of machines, and service is performed just before those failures become reality. The goal is to avoid unnecessary maintenance expenses.

Predictive maintenance is also the most difficult type of maintenance program used by manufacturers. Timing is critical because service has to be performed before the failure with sufficient warning time must be provided.

Techniques include observing machine performance, ultrasound, acoustics, thermal imaging, vibration analysis, and oil analysis.

Below are some advantages of predictive maintenance programs:

Maintenance time

This program predicts service needs. It falls under the preventative maintenance category, but service is only performed when it is justified by the potential for equipment or machine failure. This means less maintenance effort is needed for predictive maintenance, and the end result is a saving in time and labor.

Inventory

This is likely the least known advantage of predictive maintenance. Predictive maintenance does not require an inventory of excessive machine parts because only the parts necessary for the program are kept in stock. Emergency spare parts stock no longer exists, and this results in cost and space savings.

Safety

Skill levels of personnel performing predictive maintenance are high because these individuals have undergone training and understand the machines and equipment they are servicing. As a result of their knowledge, safety levels increase throughout the plant. This safety is critical because many manufacturers work with hazardous chemicals or operate equipment that requires high pressure or temperature. It creates a win-win situation for employees and management because employees do not go through the pain and suffering associated with injuries, and management does not pay the costs associated with workers' compensation.

Below are some disadvantages of predictive maintenance programs.

Monitoring/testing costs

Specialized monitoring and testing devices are typically expensive. They are made for a specific task, so a higher price can be charged for them. The cost might be understandable, but it is also prohibitive for some manufacturers. They either cannot or will not spend the money necessary for the equipment, so the predictive maintenance program does not function properly.

Required skills

Every employee is not capable of performing predictive maintenance tasks. In fact, the vast majority of employees are not capable of performing these tasks because they require specific skills. In addition to having mechanical skills, people who do predictive maintenance often need training in electronics, hydraulics, or thermodynamics.

Environmental effects

Some manufacturing plants have conditions that are less than ideal for the monitoring or testing devices necessary for predictive maintenance. For example, food processors with wet or cold working environments might have problems keeping these devices working properly. The same goes for the high temperatures found in foundries or smelting plants. Along the same lines, paint manufacturers are likely to have corrosive chemicals that could do damage.

Regardless of the way the damage is done, monitoring or testing devices that are not working properly will not provide accurate information. This means calculations could be inaccurate, and the entire predictive maintenance program is jeopardized. Since it is difficult for some manufacturers to avoid destructive work environments, it is understandable why they choose not to implement this type of program.

Now you understand some of the advantages and disadvantages of predictive maintenance. This program is beneficial for many manufacturers because it analyzes machinery and predicts when it will fail. This information is then used to perform service before the failure occurs while housing fewer parts and maintaining lower labor costs for maintenance personnel. However, people need specific skills to be employed as predictive maintenance technicians, and the type of work environment can affect the data collected.

Next, let's move into a discussion on a type of program that addresses machinery and equipment failures after they occur. That program is known as corrective maintenance.

Corrective maintenance

This is the most common type of maintenance program in manufacturing plants. It is a completely reactive program, and it is necessary because equipment and machines will break down at some point. Machines cannot be expected to run forever, and constant use at full capacity typically shortens that life span.

Unfortunately, corrective maintenance is often the only type of maintenance program available in a manufacturing facility....with no predictive or preventative programs to support it. Many times this is due to cost because smaller manufacturers cannot afford to sacrifice the resources necessary to set up predictive or preventive programs. However, sometimes corrective maintenance stands alone simply because organizations do not want to invest the necessary time and effort to establish other programs.

Corrective maintenance does wonderful things for equipment and machinery repair, but it needs help. Without some type of support, corrective maintenance programs can become very expensive in a relatively short period of time. Plant managers need to decide what type of support will be given, and that is typically not an easy task because every facility faces unique challenges.

Below are some advantages of corrective maintenance programs.

Initial investment

Corrective maintenance does not require the planning, time, or effort required for preventative and predictive programs. This is because corrective maintenance does not address problems before they occur; it simply reacts to issues at the time of failure. This is advantageous for manufacturers because they save on resources. In short, there is a savings on the initial investment for manufacturers that choose corrective maintenance as their only maintenance program.

Expenses

Corrective maintenance delays expenses. These expenses include the services and checks performed under preventative and predictive maintenance programs. This means machines and equipment can function for extended periods of time with little or no maintenance. This strategy is particularly beneficial for manufacturers looking for short-term return on investment, such as that expected from machinery or equipment needed for a specific purpose. For example, a toy manufacturing company might need a machine to stitch stuffed animals for two months until they implement an entirely new process. Management does not want to put time and money into the maintenance of this machine unless it completely fails. Even if the machine breaks down, it will be "quick-fixed" or temporarily repaired because it will not be needed for the long term. In this case, the short-term return justifies corrective maintenance being the only program in effect.

Profitability

Profit is a major reason that most manufacturers are in business, and higher profits can be made by organizations that prefer to react to maintenance issues as they occur. They are willing to forego using any type of predictive or preventative programs to make more money. Savings from labor, supplies, and parts all lead to higher profitability...and a happier management team.

Below are some disadvantages of corrective maintenance programs.

Predictability

As most manufacturers are aware, this is likely the biggest disadvantage of a corrective maintenance program. Maintenance personnel do not know when equipment or machinery will fail, and that can cause a variety of different problems. For example, parts might need to be ordered, thereby delaying the repairs necessary to get production running. Additionally, outside service might need to be called in for issues that cannot be resolved by plant personnel...and that service is typically quite expensive. When these problems mount, the cost of the corrective maintenance program can far exceed that of a program that had preventative measures in place.

Efficiency

Efficiency is important for every production-oriented facility because increasing it helps keep costs down and maximizes productivity. Unfortunately, corrective maintenance programs do little for efficiency. The major goal of corrective maintenance is to keep equipment and machinery operating, but optimal levels of operation are not necessarily part of that goal. When optimal levels are not achieved, equipment and machinery do not reach their potential...and the resulting lack of efficiency causes a decline in productivity.

Urgency

As has already been stated in this book, corrective maintenance programs do not prevent problems. This makes the likelihood of problems much more probable, and those problems need to be addressed immediately when they affect production. As might be expected, most machinery problems hinder production, so repairs need to be made with no time to waste. Unfortunately, this type of environment creates a wealth of stress for maintenance personnel and managers...and that is why urgency is a negative associated with corrective maintenance.

Plant managers need to have an understanding of all three types of maintenance programs discussed above because they are responsible for making sure the machines in their facilities are maintained and operational. They need to decide which type of programs will be implemented and how much money can be spent on those programs. This task can be challenging, but it is critical to minimize costs and maximize production capabilities.

Engineering

In manufacturing plants, engineering is related to maintenance, but it deserves a separate section of discussion because maintenance people are most concerned with servicing and repairing machines while engineers tend to focus on designing and building them.

Specific branches of engineering are described below. Plant management personnel need to have an understanding of each of these branches because they are responsible for overseeing them. Fortunately, many plant managers have engineering backgrounds, so the work performed by professional engineers comes naturally to them.

Mechanical engineering (ME)

Mechanical engineers have a variety of different responsibilities where they apply their education, natural ability, and work experience. This is understandable based on the relatively high wages these individuals are paid in exchange for their services. They are expected to provide a return-on-investment, and that return-on-investment starts with responsibility.

The following are specific responsibilities of mechanical engineers in manufacturing facilities:

Research and development

This is often assigned to mechanical engineers employed in higher education, but research and development (R&D) is also a focal point in some companies. In fact, organizations that are heavily involved in manufacturing often have an entire department devoted to R&D. However, regardless of the setting, R&D is something that MEs are usually responsible for at some point in their careers.

In higher education, R&D mechanical engineers often apply theoretical concepts in laboratory settings. This leads to discoveries and innovations that drive technology in business. However, the downside is the fact that not all laboratory findings have real-world application.

In industry, MEs with R&D responsibilities usually come up with new ideas for machines and other mechanical systems. They start with an idea or concept and try to bring it from the laboratory to the production floor where it can be utilized to lower costs and raise efficiency.

Equipment and machinery design

This is one of the most common responsibilities of mechanical engineers. They design equipment and machinery with a variety of different factors in mind including quality, safety, cost, and efficiency. These factors are broken down as follows:

> *Quality* - Quality refers to the specifications of products, equipment, or machinery. If ranges or tolerances are specified, then mechanical engineering personnel are responsible for meeting them.

> *Safety* - This refers to the safety of the personnel operating equipment or machinery. Various safeguards need to be

put in place so operators do not get hurt. Without these safeguards in place, injuries can be very serious....and even fatal in some situations.

Cost - Cost refers to the money needed to get the equipment or machinery from the design phase to the shop floor. Essentially, it is the labor and materials required to make the project successful. Cost also refers to the time and effort required to run and maintain the machine once it is operational.

Efficiency- Mechanical engineers need to get involved to make sure the equipment or machinery is meeting productivity expectations. Efficiency is very important in production-based facilities...and that is why MEs are employed in manufacturing plants.

Equipment and machinery modification

As noted above, efficiency is the responsibility of mechanical engineers. If equipment and machinery are not meeting performance expectations, then they need to be modified. Sometimes this can be done in process, and other times it means going back to the drawing board. Either way, MEs are responsible for performance modifications.

Process design

Some people assume that a lack of efficiency is due to the design of equipment or machinery. This is sometimes true, but it is not always an accurate assumption. The problem can be the process itself...and mechanical engineers are responsible for improving that process. They make changes to increase efficiency and lower costs based on observations and calculations.

Training

It should not come as a surprise that employees need to be trained on various operational and safety aspects of the equipment and machinery they operate. When this need arises, mechanical engineers are often the trainers because they were involved with that equipment and machinery from conception to implementation. They understand what needs to be done for safe and efficient operation, and they can answer any employee questions.

Project management

Most mechanical engineers are responsible for some type of project management. They oversee new production lines being implemented, procedures being changed, or expansions of workspaces. Regardless of the type of project, they are responsible for seeing it through to completion and this involves the management of people and processes. In this capacity, they also work as a liaison with outside contractors to ensure the project is finished in a timely and efficient manner.

Electrical engineering (EE)

Electrical engineers have a variety of job responsibilities that require them to find economical and timely solutions to problems with many different variables. They need to be able to apply theory, think rationally, perform multiple tasks, make decisions, and work with others. It is difficult to list every job duty of EEs, but their major responsibilities are as follows:

Research and development

R&D electrical engineers are often employed in higher education, but R&D is also conducted in organizations.

Automotive suppliers and manufacturers are good examples of companies that employ EEs in R&D. These companies often build multi-million dollar laboratories designed solely for EE research. In these labs, electrical engineers often use computer design software. They start with an idea or concept, build prototypes, prepare reports and other documentation, and present their findings to higher management.

Data analysis

This ranks at the top of responsibilities for electrical engineers because they need to be capable of evaluating data received from components and systems to apply their knowledge and make decisions. Data analysis helps EEs design programs that create new products or solve problems encountered by employees in other areas of the organization. This makes everyone's job easier, and it saves time and money. That being said, people who do not possess data analysis skills probably should not be electrical engineers.

Computer-assisted design

Electrical engineers often work on projects. As part of the process, they typically use computer-assisted design (CAD) to visualize their ideas. These blueprints are important because they show flaws and prevent projects from being continued when problems show that they will not work. CAD allows EEs to efficiently put their ideas on paper or a screen, and it is a great tool for implementing specifications and adhering to other project requirements.

Equipment or machinery modification

This is an important responsibility for electrical engineers because they understand what machinery and equipment are capable of doing from an electrical standpoint. They observe operators in action and ask them questions pertaining to their jobs. After processing this information, they apply their knowledge and modify equipment or machinery to correct the problem.

Training

Some electrical engineering functions, such as CAD work or data analysis, are done strictly by EEs. However, this does not exempt them from training duties. Production employees need to be trained on operational and safety aspects of the machinery they operate, and EEs are the best instructors because they can answer any questions related to the subject matter.

Project management

Electrical engineers work on many different projects in manufacturing plants. They test products, research cost-effective solutions, record and interpret data, and communicate their findings to customers and higher management. Regardless of the type of project EEs are assigned, they are responsible for seeing it through to completion...and this involves efficiently managing people and processes.

Chemical engineering (CE)

Chemical engineers perform a variety of different job tasks, and the responsibilities associated with those tasks can vary extensively from one engineer to another. For example, some CHEs work only with specific processes such as polymerization, while others focus on entire fields such as biomedical engineering. They are further divided within these areas because some CHEs do research while others work on manufacturing problems. Those who work in manufacturing fall under the supervision of plant managers and their job responsibilities include the following:

Safety

Safety is a responsibility of many chemical engineers because they work in environments that manufacture hazardous chemicals. CHEs develop procedures for working with these chemicals based on their understanding of chemical reactions and the potential for injurious or lethal situations. If something is not safe, CHEs work to find alternative processes, raw materials, or chemistry to reduce the risk of injury. The importance of this responsibility should never be underestimated because it prevents humans from being harmed or, in extreme situations, killed.

Product development

Chemical engineers are often involved in product development. Interestingly, they sometimes find success by taking a backward approach. They are well trained for finding more efficient ways of doing things, so their road to product development often starts with defining better processes. They identify workable solutions to process problems and then work backward to develop unique products that are safe and cost-effective. This is not a new concept for scientists and, in reality, CHEs make up some of the best scientists in the world.

Evaluation

Solutions to problems in manufacturing are often found by chemical engineers. They troubleshoot by evaluating situations with a "think before act" mentality. They analyze equipment and processes first, and then they make decisions based on their education and experience. This evaluation procedure is similar to that used by other engineers...with one difference. That difference is the fact that CHEs always find solutions to problems with safety and environmental concerns in mind. If the end result has safety violations or negative environmental impact, then CHEs work toward a better alternative.

Design

This refers to process design rather than product design. Process design is the centerpiece of chemical engineering because it extracts and utilizes all components in the field. Because of this, CHEs are often charged with developing new processes that resolve existing issues in manufacturing facilities. They implement plans with procedures that coincide with equipment layout for maximum safety and efficiency. In terms of design, CHEs are usually the best employees that organizations have to offer.

Training

Yes, training is again mentioned as a responsibility of a specific type of engineering. Chemical engineers usually conduct some type of training, and it is often geared toward safety. CHEs are responsible for the safety of personnel at all times, and they invest substantial time and effort into preventing work-related injuries. Their training efforts are important...especially for employees working with dangerous or hazardous chemicals in manufacturing plants.

As mentioned earlier, many plant managers have engineering backgrounds so they understand the roles that engineers play in manufacturing facilities. However, regardless of their level of understanding, plant managers must be able to oversee engineering departments to assure their effectiveness and efficiency.

Supply chain management (SCM)

Manufacturers need to purchase raw materials and supplies to produce finished products. Not surprisingly, those raw materials and supplies do not magically show up at the doorstep...they have to be ordered by purchasing agents in a timely fashion at the best possible price.

Purchasing agents, also known as buyers, follow designated company strategies when making buying decisions. They often adhere to a just-in-time philosophy where raw materials and supplies are brought in only when needed. Excessive inventory needs to be avoided due to the money that gets tied up, and all decisions are made with cost in mind.

In the past, purchasing for manufacturers was primarily done by lower-level employees. A manager told a clerical worker what was needed, and the order was placed. However, strategic purchasing has made this process a relic of the past that will likely never return. Purchasing is now done by management personnel who have a great deal of authority and responsibility...and plant managers are their bosses.

Supply chain management is a controlled system where organizations along the entire supply chain work together to produce and deliver the best possible products at the lowest cost. Shared resources are used to assure purchasing, production, and distribution are effective and efficient while meeting established quality standards. This gives producers of products a competitive advantage in today's lean manufacturing environment.

In the global marketplace, many manufacturers rely on outsourcing and suppliers to do some of their production. This works well for getting products made, but reliance on others brings about quality concerns. Those concerns are the reason that the modern era supply chain management came into play.

In manufacturing, SCM manages the flow of goods from the purchasing of raw materials to the delivery of finished products...including the storage and inventorying of all stock. The plan is to synchronize supply and demand while monitoring and controlling all activities along the chain. Based on this plan, it is rather obvious that good communication is critical at all levels.

SCM utilizes logistics, engineering, operations, and technology to accomplish manufacturing goals and objectives. For example, inventory levels of raw materials and finished products must always be accessible for reordering, production scheduling, and fulfillment of customer orders. Modern barcoding technology has made this possible because it can receive information about inventory that includes past and present locations, quantities, and future destinations.

Essentially, supply chain management in manufacturing can be broken down into three major phases as follows:

Strategical

This is the planning stage. A road map for the SCM needs to be developed, and supply chain partners need to be identified. Where, when, and how will the finished products be manufactured? Who will supply the raw materials? Is another company going to manufacture part or all of the finished products? Where will the finished products be warehoused? These questions need to be answered during the strategical phase, and those answers are best achieved using collaboration from all partners in the chain. For example, companies need input from each other to figure out what makes the most sense from a logistical standpoint and which organization is most capable of manufacturing specific products.

Tactical

This is the execution stage. It involves putting the plan into effect and finalizing the details. What quantity of raw materials and finished products will be inventoried? What are the costs associated with raw materials and finished products? What are the quality specifications for raw materials and finished products? These questions need to be answered during the tactical phase, and those answers are best achieved using collaboration from all partners in the chain. For example, it might seem like the quality specifications should be set by the manufacturers, but they need input from their suppliers for realistic expectations. Along the same lines, suppliers need to communicate with manufacturers about cost so the best economical solutions can be obtained.

Operational

This is the maintenance stage. It is where the day-to-day activities are managed to ensure the supply chain runs efficiently and effectively. It entails all plant activities including purchasing, receiving, production, inventory, storage, and shipping. What types of raw materials need to be ordered? What types of raw materials need to be inventoried? What types of finished products need to be manufactured? What types of finished products need to be inventoried? These questions need to be answered during the operational phase, and those answers are best achieved using collaboration from all partners in the chain. For example, manufacturers need distributors to help them make production decisions, and they need to communicate with suppliers about fulfilling raw material needs.

Plant managers are responsible for overseeing supply chain management in manufacturing facilities. They need to understand the flow of goods from the raw material stage to the finished product stage and this requires having the right people and procedures in place to make sure that flow is continuous with minimal interruptions. This task can be challenging, but most facilities have competent personnel in place to handle the day-to-day activities and interactions so the plant managers only need to get involved when serious problems arise.

Planning

Planning is a management action designed to establish priorities, allocate resources, implement change, and guide an organization toward defined goals. It stems from a vision of where the organization is now and where it wants to be in the future. In manufacturing facilities, this vision often comes from the plant managers who know that there is truth in the saying, "those who fail to plan, plan to fail."

Planning starts with a defined purpose. What is expected to be accomplished? What are the goals? Next, an analysis of the situation needs to be made to determine the people and resources required for tor the tasks that need to be completed to accomplish the goals. Once the purpose is defined and an analysis is made, it is time to implement some type of strategy. That strategy must utilize the resources to provide a path that leads to goal accomplishment.

Plant managers know that planning is needed because it forces people to look at an overview of the path they are going to take to reach designated goals. This can pinpoint areas that might not work or do not make sense based on organizational strengths and weaknesses. Milestones are achievements made as the plan progresses. As employees reach these achievements, they are motivated to keep working toward the ultimate goals of the plan.

Plans should be used whenever there is a goal in mind that takes time and effort to attain. For example, a plan is not necessary for an assembly line employee whose goal is to go to the drinking fountain and get a drink of water. However, a plan is necessary if the goal is for everyone in the plant to have a drinking fountain within 200 feet of their work area.

Three basic types of planning are as follows:

Strategical

Strategical plans apply to the entire organization, establish a mission, define short-term and long-term goals, and provide a framework for employees to expand upon. High-ranking employees design and implement these plans, and the objectives are supported by lower-level employees using tactical planning. In short, these plans are a roadmap for taking an organization from where it is to where it wants to be in the future.

Organizational example

Carmella is the plant manager of a taco shell manufacturing company. She has established a goal of expanding the company's brand from regional to national in the next five years. She wants to do this by adding $80,000,000 in sales growth to the foodservice (restaurants, hotels, and institutions) segment of the business.

Carmella has hired brokers in New York, Chicago, Miami, Seattle, and San Diego to represent the taco shell product line. She has also secured the option of renting another production plant if the company's current two plants cannot handle the increase in volume.

A framework for the growth of the taco shell manufacturer has been provided by Carmella. She has hired people to meet sales projections, and she will be able to meet the production demand that results from the increased sales. The mission of the company has been established and is moving forward thanks to the strategical planning of Carmella.

Tactical

Tactical plans support strategic plans in lower-level areas of the organization. They focus on the way specific divisions or departments put strategic plans into action.

Tactical plans often have short-term goals because they are not nearly as encompassing as strategic plans. In short, managers take departmental actions based on the goals and objectives of the strategic plan.

Organizational example

Jessica is the plant manager of a uniform manufacturing and supply company. In this capacity, she supervises 21 drivers who ensure that uniforms are delivered to customers on a bi-weekly basis.

The uniform company has set a strategic plan for reducing costs by 15 percent over the next two years. Based on this objective, Jessica implements a tactical plan by reorganizing routes so that drivers no longer deliver uniforms outside of a 50-mile radius of their first stop. This means the company has to eliminate some distant customers, but the savings in gas and driver labor justifies the loss in sales.

Jessica's tactical plan of reducing gas and labor expenses supports the strategic plan of reducing organizational costs. Her plan goes into effect and her short-term goal of reducing costs is realized within the first few weeks.

Operational

Operational plans are those which occur every day in organizations all over the world. They are typically conducted by managers to achieve the goals of their department and, ultimately, the organization.

Operational plans usually have an operational goal. For example, an appliance manufacturing plant might plan to work two shifts, six days per week for the next eight weeks with a goal of producing 350 refrigerators and 300 stoves.

Operational plans often work to support strategic plans that are the goal of the organization. In the appliance example, the strategic plan might be to run a month-long sale on refrigerators and stoves. Based on this, inventory of these two items needs to be built to levels to support that sale....and that is the reason for the operational plan of producing 350 refrigerators and 300 stoves.

Operational plans are often broken down into two categories:

Single usage

These types of operational plans are designed for one-time use only. Since they are specified in nature and time frame, they typically have a budget associated with them.

Organizational example

Jack is the plant manager of a baseball glove manufacturing company. He wants to hold an exhibition at a local sports arena to show people what the company has to offer. The goal of the exhibition is to push the value of the gloves to children.

Jack sets a budget of $10,000 for the project. The exhibition is an operational plan designed for single usage with the goal of attracting customers.

Continuous usage

These types of operational plans are designed for non-stop usage. They are typically created one time and used for getting consistent messages across to many people.

Organizational example

Bugweitzer Candy is a German candy maker that has been in business for over 100 years. They pride themselves on using the same recipes for generations, and those recipes include the mint-flavored chocolate bars they sell during the holidays.

There is a specific procedure in place for making these bars. The same process and ingredients have been used since the company was founded, and employees are not allowed to make any changes unless they are put in writing by management.

Bugweitzer's procedure for mint-flavored chocolate bars is a continuous plan that is designed for ongoing usage. Modification might need to be made at times, but the goal is to produce the same product year after year.

Contingent

Contingent plans are essentially plans for alternative action if the original plan is not successful or proves to be inadequate. This can result from a variety of different reasons including new management, regulatory changes, customer requirements, economic issues, or just poor planning. Regardless of the reason, changes in circumstances can warrant plans ineffective, and this is why alternatives should be developed and ready to implement at a monument's notice.

Organizational example

Randy is the plant manager of Winkendale Furniture Manufacturing Company. The company has set a strategic goal of becoming the biggest leather-upholstered couch and chair manufacturer in Canada. They have a time frame of three years to reach this goal, and they are currently at the end of year one.

Due to unforeseen circumstances, beef prices have risen dramatically in the past three months causing leather to double in price. Furniture manufacturers have been forced to raise their leather upholstered furniture prices substantially, and some have discontinued items in their leather lines.

The increased prices of leather couches and chairs cause Randy to abandon Winkendale's strategic plan for becoming the biggest leather-upholstered couch and chair manufacturer in Canada. Fortunately, the company had a contingent plan as a backup. The goal of the contingent plan is for the company to become one of the top three manufacturers of couches and chairs in Canada, and Randy decides to put that plan into action.

Inventory control

Inventory control is a system that accounts for all items, raw materials, and finished products, in stock at a manufacturer. It determines the location and quantity of these items so employees know what is on hand and where to get it. Without effective inventory control programs, manufacturers have difficulty stocking the items necessary to make their products. When this happens, orders are not filled and customers are not happy.

Inventory control is needed for a variety of reasons, but astute plant managers are aware of the major ones listed below.

- It ensures that finished product stock is maintained at a sufficient level. Too much inventory results in unnecessary costs and too little inventory results in unfulfilled customer orders. Inventory is expensive, but so are lost customer sales...so there needs to be a balance.
- It can be used to track raw materials or finished product usage. When an item goes out of stock, people who order it are notified so they can replenish the supply.
- It establishes reorder levels for raw materials and finished products. Reorder warnings are issued when inventory dips below designated levels.
- It detects theft, damage, and other losses. If inventory is missing but nothing was sold or produced, then there is a problem.

Smart plant managers also know that inventory control programs do not always work properly. While the list of reasons for failure can be quite extensive, some of the more significant ones include:

Lack of planning - It is not uncommon for manufacturers to spend large amounts of money on inventory control software only to find that it does not meet their expectations. This happens for the following reasons:

- Management does plan for operating the system once it is live. They assume the software will run itself because they have invested a lot of money into it. The software will work, but management needs to understand what is needed to make it perform properly.
- Management does not plan for putting the right people in charge of the system. They assume employees will "fill in as needed" and take responsibility for aspects of the program that apply to their jobs.
- Management does not plan for a complete switch over to the new program. Some employees refuse to let go of old inventory control methods unless they are forced to do so. They do not trust or like the new software, so they keep doing things the way they have been doing them....and never learn the new program. Cut off dates need to be set in advance and enforced.

Regardless of the reason, planning is essential for getting inventory control systems to work effectively and produce valid information. Once again, plant managers must be aware that, "those who fail to plan, plan to fail."

Lack of physical inventorying - Sharp plant managers are aware that this is probably the biggest reason for the failure of inventory control programs. Think of the old adage, "garbage in" equals "garbage out" because it is very applicable to inventory control. In fact, it is possible that this saying gained popularity among inventory control professionals.

If the people doing physical inventorying do not enter accurate information, the system will not work. For example, assume 1000 boxes of pencils are in stock at a warehouse. However, the person inventorying this item only enters 600 boxes because he missed three pallets that are in a different location of the building.

This error causes a domino effect of other errors that cannot be corrected until the pencils are correctly counted. When customers buy pencils, the inventory is inaccurate...as is the case when new pencils are ordered. Re-order levels are also inaccurate, so too many or too few pencils could be kept on hand. Add this to the fact that inventory costs are wrong, and the end result is a major fiasco...all because inaccurate numbers were entered during physical inventory. Unfortunately, these inaccuracies can negatively impact the bottom lines of organizations.

Lack of customer understanding - Manufacturers that do not understand the inventory needs of their customers will not have a successful inventory control program. There must be a basic understanding of customer orders, and this is best done by tracking trends.

For example, a meat processor's inventory control computer program is designated to reorder turkeys when inventory goes down to 500 birds. This assures a two-week supply will always be on hand. However, the program does not know that 80 percent of the turkeys are purchased two weeks before Thanksgiving...and the company runs out of birds at a critical time. Employees are upset with the computer program, but it is not the problem. Management needs to understand customer needs during this holiday and appropriately adjust reordering levels based on those needs.

Manufacturing personnel become upset when inventory programs do not perform as expected. However, often the program is not at fault...as shown in the example above. The fault, quite simply, stems from the people in charge. If this is the case, then plant managers need to step in and make changes.

Plant managers also need to be aware of problems that result when manufacturing inventory control programs do not work. These problems include:

- Products go missing without being noticed. This prevents mistakes and theft from being detected and rectified.
- Product shortages result from inventory trends not being noticed. This results in unhappy customers.
- Product overstocking is not detected. This results in money being unnecessarily spent and tied up.
- Product overstocking makes storage space an issue.

- Time and money are spent trying to resolve inventory problems.
- Shipping and transportation delays result from a lack of accurate information.

Based on the above, it is fairly obvious that inventory control systems need to work properly or there will be consequences. Plant managers are responsible for overseeing the efficient running of these systems by making sure that the right people and procedures are in place.

Plant managers also need to understand the goals of inventory systems. These goals can be quite complex and diverse, but the major ones are as follows.

Track finished products

This is the most commonly known and understood goal of inventory control. Finished products need to be stored and accounted for to meet customer demand. Inventory control programs track the quantity and types of finished products in stock so manufacturers can be confident that they have enough to fulfill orders.

Believe it or not, many manufacturers are unaware of their finished product inventory. They have disorganized warehouses where products are not kept in common bays or designated areas. They also do a poor job of physical inventorying, so quantities being entered are wrong making every calculation that follows inaccurate. Add the fact that these companies have even less knowledge of their finished products that are

70

stored offsite, and it is relatively easy to see why they have difficulty tracking their inventory.

Finished product accuracy is a major reason why manufacturers need inventory control. The complexity, location, and quantity of items produced by some of these companies indicate the need for computerized programs with relevant software. However, manual systems will work if the proper amount of time and effort are put forth. Either way, accurate information on finished products is important for organizational growth and survival, and that is why trend tracking is a major goal of inventory control programs.

Track raw materials

Manufacturers need raw materials to produce finished products. These raw materials are used at various points of the production process, so they must be kept on hand and stored in the facility.

The inventorying of raw materials is similar to that of finished products, except for the fact that the customer is the company itself. Raw materials are only used internally to build finished products, so one department "sells" or transfers them to another during the production process.

Quantities, location, and usage of all raw materials need to be tracked for cost and production purposes. This is done using inventory control programs, and that makes tracking raw materials an important goal of those programs.

Track trends

Organizations that turnover raw materials and finished products need inventory control for many different reasons, and competitiveness is one of those reasons. Inventory systems help manufacturers remain competitive because they generate a wealth of beneficial information. Some of that information, such as sales of individual products, is useful for tracking trends.

Unfortunately, many organizations fail to do a good job of tracking trends, and this gives their competition an advantage. In manufacturing, trends are important because they indicate the need for production during specific periods of time. For example, an ice cream manufacturer understands that sales are higher in the summer, so management must schedule production accordingly. However, before that scheduling can be done, some questions need to be answered. How much sugar, cream, cocoa, vanilla, corn syrup, and ice cream base should be kept on hand to make the ice cream? What type of cartons are needed for the ice cream and how many must be stored? How much of each flavor of ice cream should be ready for sale to customers? These questions can be answered with inventory control. Records allow the ice cream maker to look back on summers of previous years to see what raw materials were on hand and what finished products were produced, stored, and shipped. After a few calculations, raw materials can be purchased and production can be scheduled with confidence.

In short, trends help manufacturers meet customer demands while making their production processes efficient and effective. This makes them more competitive and explains why trend tracking is an important goal of inventory control.

Prevent theft

Leaders of organizations do not like to think that their employees would steal from them, but reality shows that some will if opportunities are present. In fact, most inventory theft comes from employees...and manufacturing plants are always under threat for this type of illegal behavior.

In manufacturing facilities, theft is possible in many different areas of production. Products do not have to be finished for people to steal, and that is one reason raw materials are accounted for continuously. Unscrupulous individuals stop at nothing to make money at the expense of others, and manufacturers are preferred targets because they have so many different items in inventory that can be sold for pure profit.

Theft prevention is critical to leaders of organizations, and this makes it a significant goal of inventory control systems. Since workplaces will likely never completely rid themselves of dishonest employees, this goal will likely never disappear or diminish in importance.

Prevent overages

At first glance, raw material and/or finished product overages in manufacturing plants might not seem like a major issue. After all, the material or product will get used...it is just a matter of time. Although this type of thinking might appear reasonable, it is completely wrong because stock overages cost organizations money. In fact, stock overages can cost large companies millions of dollars a year for purchasing and storage of items that are simply not needed. Additionally, space is required that could be utilized much more efficiently.

A major goal of inventory control is to prevent stock overages to save manufacturers money. In this respect, inventory control systems minimize costs and help organizations become more economically stable.

Prevent shortages

Raw material or finished product shortages are fairly common problems in manufacturing facilities. People order wrong quantities, order correct quantities at the wrong times, or simply do not order at all because they forgot or were unaware that stock was needed.

A major reason for shortages is uncertainty. Purchasing agents and salespeople are not sure how to forecast product sales, and this causes them to underestimate.

In the end, demand exceeds supply...and the end result is unhappy customers because their orders are not filled.

Effective inventory control systems prevent shortages from occurring in manufacturers. They provide information that helps people make calculated decisions about lead times and quantities of orders. This prevents mistakes from happening that hinder production and produce dissatisfied customers.

Stock shortages create headaches for manufacturers, and that is why preventing them is a goal of inventory control programs.

Inventory control systems show what happens to raw materials and finished products. They track raw materials used to manufacture finished products, locations where finished products were delivered, customers who made purchases, and prices paid for transactions. This information can then be used by management to verify that their company is performing effectively and efficiently. In short, inventory control systems ensure accuracy, and that accuracy is ultimately the responsibility of the plant managers who oversee the facility operations.

Packaging

People who are not directly involved in the manufacturing of products probably do not think about packaging. After all, they make purchases for the product inside...not the surrounding packaging material. They usually do not notice that the packaging of a product is high quality because they expect it to be that way. However, they will notice a problem with the packaging very quickly if it does do what it is supposed to do. For example, a broken tamper-resistant seal on an aspirin bottle usually results in consumers refusing to buy that product. Those consumers search for a good seal, purchase a similar product, or purchase the same product elsewhere.

Plant managers must realize that packaging rests on meeting consumer demands, and they have to organize packaging-related processes based on those demands. They need to take into account the following four major factors:

Technological advances

Technology affects virtually every aspect of manufacturing in some way, shape, or form...and packaging is no exception. Durability, strength, tear resistance, tamper resistance, oxygen permeability, and moisture permeability are all examples of packaging characteristics that have been impacted by technology. These features and many others continue to improve with technological advancements, but the largest impact will likely be the way these packages are manufactured after the advancements have been implemented.

The biggest manufacturing advancement in terms of technology is 3D printing. This process has the potential to completely transform the packaging world by printing materials on demand. At the moment, 3D printing is too costly to be used by the majority of packaging manufacturers. However, like any other new technology, the price will eventually go down as technology improves. When that happens, manufacturers will use this process in many different ways including individualizing packaging for the masses. This might sound impossible, but it is not. It will happen, and it is not that far off...and plant managers need to be ready to implement the required changes.

Regulatory intervention

Plant managers must understand that due to consumer demands, regulatory agencies are requiring more from packaging. For example, products from food manufacturers require detailed ingredient statements and nutritional facts panels. All ingredients need to be listed with nothing hidden from the consumer, and specific nutritional information is required.

There are also regulations regarding the chemical make-up of packaging materials. Materials considered to be carcinogenic or dangerous in any way to people's health are being banned regularly, and plant managers must have the ability to react.

Last, but certainly not least, physical packaging standards need to be implemented. Strength testing is required to assure packaging material can hold up under normal conditions. For example, a corrugated box for a 50 lb barbecue grill might need to show that the handles do not tear under the stress of the weight when it is being carried by a person. In short, the government is involved with packaging, and manufacturers have no choice other than to conform.

Environmental concerns

No industry can escape the monitoring of environmental watchdogs. These scrutinizing groups are becoming stronger and more vocal, and they show no indication of backing down. Unfortunately, this scrutiny negatively impacts the packaging industry since a major focus is put on the recycling of packaging materials. Plant managers need to understand that manufacturers need to invest time and effort into creating recyclable materials that meet the demands of environmentalists.

Cost

Environmental concerns, technology, regulatory intervention, and consumer demands combine to make packaging costs higher than they have ever been in the past. Plant managers must understand that this cost cannot always be passed on to consumers, so other avenues need to be explored to absorb it. One such avenue involves condensing or concentrating products. Concentrated products require less packaging material, thereby lowering the unit cost. An example includes concentrated laundry soap.

Another avenue involves lighter materials. At first glance, this might seem like it would do nothing, but plant managers need to realize that it has three distinct benefits. First, it reduces the use of raw materials. If a package is 20 percent lighter using the same material, then 20 percent less of that material is used, and the cost is lowered. Second, lighter packaging saves storage space. More packages can be warehoused in the same amount of warehouse space. Third, lighter packaging saves transportation costs. More units can be shipped for the same amount of money, thereby lowering the overall transportation costs.

Warehousing

Warehouses are areas where products are stored after they are packaged and before they are sold to customers. They are a necessary part of many manufacturing facilities because those facilities need inventory to fill customer orders.

Warehouses are typically very structured. They have designated areas for every product so employees have an idea of where they need to go when they fill customer orders. For example, a furniture manufacturing warehouse has bedroom furniture in one area and office furniture in another area. Additionally, most warehouses store the oldest products in the front to assure proper rotation. For example, a sausage manufacturer would have hot dogs with a sell-by date of February 17th in front of the hot dogs with a sell-by date of March 4th.

Products in inventory are often designated by stock-keeping units (also known as SKU). SKUs contain product numbers, product types, and product descriptions. This allows employees to search by barcode labels using scanning guns, which is much easier and faster than visually searching for products.

Not surprisingly, supervisors of warehouses manage them in a variety of different ways. They often operate using methods that they are most comfortable with, but those methods are not necessarily the most efficient. Perceptive plant managers are aware that the most efficient methods involve best practices, and some of the more important practices are described below.

Set-up

Without proper setup, best practices that follow will be hindered. Some aspects of this are simple such as making sure bays store products vertically rather than horizontally, keeping like products together, and providing room for jacks and Hi-Los to operate. However, other pieces of the set-up puzzle require thorough analysis such as deciding which type of software to purchase, defining specific personnel responsibilities, and mapping out the process flow from receiving to shipping.

Regardless of the amount of time and effort put into the set-up, smart plant managers know that it must be done correctly for the smooth implementation of other best practices. In short, setup is critical because it functions as the planning phase of warehousing.

Receiving

Receiving marks the beginning of the warehouse process. It is where the product comes into the storage area for shipping. Once products enter the warehouse, they become the responsibility of warehouse personnel. Production employees have done their jobs, and products move to their final destination before they reach customers.

Documentation is necessary to show what products have been moved from the packaging department to the warehouse. A log should be maintained to show what has been received. This log is useful for warehouse personnel, but it can also be used by employees in other departments. Accountants, inventory control personnel, and salespeople all use this information to help them do their jobs better. Accountants assign different costs and values to finished products in storage, inventory control personnel move products from in-process to finished, and salespeople know they have finished products available to sell to customers.

Products that are wrongly packaged, labeled, or coded need to be stopped at receiving and sent back for corrective action. This action puts the responsibility back on the shoulders of packaging personnel and prevents customers from becoming upset about faulty products.

In short, plant managers need to understand that receiving cannot be taken lightly because it is very important for organizations. It is the last internal check before products are transported, and it could prevent problems from occurring once those products are in the field.

Flow

This refers to the movement of products once they are in the warehouse. It requires employees who know how to drive powered jacks and forklifts and are certified for doing so. Most states offer powered industrial lift written tests that certify operators. Operators who answer questions incorrectly simply need to be shown the correct answers and sign off that they understand where their mistakes were made.

Unfortunately, understanding how to properly operate powered jacks and forklifts is a simple aspect of best practices for inventory flow. It is much more difficult to accurately pick orders for customers. Order picking involves finding the product, selecting the correct amount, and making sure the oldest product is selected first. A FIFO (first in, first out) system is helpful for properly selecting the rotating stock, but it does not guarantee success. Many problems in warehouses stem from orders that were not picked properly or stock that was not rotated. Erroneous order picking leads to inaccurate inventory numbers that negatively impact many people's jobs. Scanning guns and software programs make this process easier, but they are also not foolproof. In short, employees who pick orders need to be able to think and reason.

Shipping

After the product has been picked, it is moved to the shipping dock. It remains on the dock until it is loaded on a truck for transport to the customer or distributor. This might seem like a fairly cut-and-dry process, but some concerns require the implementation of best practices due to the potential for the following:

Theft

Shrewd plant managers understand that dishonest people are always looking for opportunities to steal, and shipping docks often provide those opportunities. Products that are temporarily stored on docks tend to go unwatched, and thieves take advantage of that lack of monitoring. They steal individual products...and they even take entire pallets of products if they are able to back their trucks into wells. Typically, products with high values are targeted by these criminals, but they will pilfer anything they can profit from.

Damage

Damage can occur for a variety of different reasons. Some products become contaminated due to malicious individuals while other products are damaged due to the careless or accidental actions of employees. Examples include puncturing a hole in an oil barrel causing it to leak all over the dock, hitting a pallet of pens with the forklift of a Hilo causing the pens to break and fall out of their boxes, or leaving meat on a dock too long causing it to spoil. All of these examples can be caused by mistakes or purposeful intent...but the point is that they can and do occur.

Loading mistakes

Product might make it all the way to the truck before a problem occurs. Examples include (1) loading the wrong amount of product on a truck and (2) putting the correct amount of product on the wrong truck. Typically, loading mistakes are accidental, but they are still a shipping concern.

Based on the potential for problems, plant managers need to understand the importance of monitoring products on shipping docks. One way to do this is to have a shipping manager who monitors all shipping related activity. This individual spends most of his or her working day on the dock floor and has a "fishbowl" office with windows that allow unrestricted viewing of all dock happenings.

Another way to safeguard products on shipping docks is to restrict shipping dock access to authorized personnel. Locked doors with codes, keys, or swipe cards can be used to restrict personnel and prevent wrongful activities. Locks also limit the number of potentially responsible people when there is a problem that needs to be investigated...especially if time stamps and names are documented every time a person unlocks a door.

The third method of monitoring involves the use of cameras. Cameras are placed at strategic points so that every inch of the receiving dock is under surveillance 24/7. Cameras serve a dual purpose. First, and foremost, they monitor all activity which means anything anyone does is filmed. The second purpose of cameras involves deterrence. When people know their actions are being monitored, they are less likely to do something that they know is wrong. In terms of theft, cameras are well worth the investment.

Safety

Good plant managers know that safety is a best practice of a warehouse that is often overlooked simply because it takes time and costs money. However, lack of safety can result in situations that require a lot of time and money. Rules should be in place to keep aisles clear, prevent riding on jacks and other horseplay, and make sure powered lift trucks are operating properly. These rules need to be enforced, and disciplinary action needs to be taken when they are broken.

As most plant managers are well aware, there is room for improvement in virtually every aspect of organizations. The "if it ain't broke, don't fix it" mentality simply does not apply to businesses that strive for growth and prosperity. This means the management and operation of warehouses get better, and specific suggestions for improvement include:

80/20 rule

This is a rather old rule that still has value in modern warehouses. It saves order picking time by designating specific areas for higher volume products. In short, 20 percent of the warehouse holds items that constitute 80 percent of all customer orders. This means order pickers are not traveling all over the warehouse to get the majority of items they pick on a normal day.

The 80/20 rule does not work for every warehouse because they all do not have an 80/20 mix of product sales. However, it can improve many different types of warehouses because it saves time, thereby making those operations more efficient.

Fewer boxes

Less is often more...especially when it comes to boxes. This suggestion is beneficial for warehouses that use many different boxes when packaging their products. Plant managers will have engineers design boxes that house multiple products, thereby reducing the number of boxes that need to be inventoried and the different types of pallet configurations required for products. In short, fewer boxes improve warehouses by saving time, creating space, and simplifying processes.

Technology

Warehouses can get better by improving technology. This technology consists of software and systems as shown below:

Software

New software for computerized devices is always being created, and much of it does wonders for improving warehousing. For example, barcoding uses software for generating accurate and reliable information. This technology allows for the tracking of raw materials to determine where they came from, where they are, where they are going, and when they need to be re-ordered.

The advantages of barcoding are error reduction and time savings. Accuracy is not dependent on human entry, and information can be inputted in a fraction of the time required by manual methods.

Systems

Conveyor systems are a simple method for improving the efficiency of warehousing. Conveyors transfer products from one area to another with much less labor when compared to manual transfer by employees. In short, they facilitate warehouse processes and can be set up relatively inexpensively. Some conveyor systems do not even need motors, relying on gravity or spinning wheels for product transfer.

Incentives

Employee incentives are a much-debated way to improve warehouses. Some people argue that incentives provide employee motivation...but others argue that they create unnecessary employee competition. However, when utilized properly incentives can be beneficial. People want to be rewarded for their efforts, and incentives provide that reward. If they work harder, they earn more money...so many people choose to work harder. This creates a win-win situation because employees increase their wages and warehouses increase their efficiency.

As you can see, plant managers can improve warehouses in several different ways. In the future, most of the changes that they implement will be financially driven, and they will require better management skills for the people in charge. These changes will include:

Less space

In terms of space, warehouses of the future will need to do more with less. This will require plant managers to think about processes and procedures before making decisions. High-performance equipment will need to be chosen, storage areas will need to be used wisely, waste will need to be reduced, and organizational efficiency will need to improve. That being said, plant managers of the future will be smarter and more adaptable than they are today. They will accept change at a moment's notice and be willing to venture into the unknown. They will enlarge their minds rather than their buildings to resolve space-related issues, and this will benefit their bottom lines.

Lower inventory

Similar to the future of warehouse space, inventories of the future will also be reduced by plant managers. Inventoried product costs money to keep on hand, and that money is not recouped until that product is sold. This will require more preparation, better forecasting, and faster reaction time on the part of managers. Based on these changes, planning will become a very important aspect of plant managers' jobs....and that importance will continue to increase as time goes on.

Reduce product weight

Plant managers understand that increased product weight adds cost to the entire warehousing process. Because of this, engineers will work to reduce the weight of products stored in warehouses. This change will make employees' jobs easier and reduce their injuries while lowering transportation costs for the organization. It will result in happier workforces in warehouses and healthier bottom lines for organizations.

Better technology

Technology was mentioned earlier as a way to improve warehousing...and that technology will be available in the future. Warehouse managers will have access to software that simplifies their jobs and saves their organizations money. This software will also reduce employee stress and make their jobs easier. In short, it will benefit every employee involved with the warehousing aspects of organizations.

Radio Frequency Identification (RFID) is an example of better technology that will be used more frequently in the future. Warehouses that move thousands of items through their faculties need inventorying systems that are more efficient than barcoding. For these companies, radio frequency identification (RFID) is the answer. Essentially, RFID uses radio waves to collect information on products and raw materials. That information gathered is similar to that collected by bar code scanners, but it can be read from several feet away. That being said, some readers are mounted on walls or ceilings as they accurately scan all items that pass by them.

The advantages of RFID are volume and readability. Large numbers of raw materials or finished products can be scanned without the necessity of hand-held units, and these scanners do not have to have a direct line of sight to register information. However, RFID has some technical issues and privacy concerns that need to be ironed out before it will be completely accepted.

In terms of RFID technology, there are no concrete regulations in effect, so one company's system might not be able to be read by another. This is especially troubling when the customers of manufacturers are unable to scan the items they are receiving. Additionally, these systems are difficult to program and there is a constant threat of information being intercepted. Based on these disadvantages, some warehouses are shying away from RFID...at least until the technology gets better and the risk for problems decreases.

Now you understand some of the major departments that plant managers oversee in manufacturing facilities. The next section discusses the management skills needed by these leaders to organize, motivate, and communicate with others in the workplace.

Management

Most people need some type of direction and motivation to perform at peak levels. This is not saying that they lack self-motivation and drive; it is merely saying that they need help to be the best they can be. Plant managers must be able to provide the support, encouragement, and guidance these individuals need to do their jobs effectively and efficiently. Without this assistance, productivity will suffer and morale will start to deteriorate. In short, plant managers need to be skilled in the areas listed below.

Motivation

Employees have often been referred to as an organization's greatest assets. This is because, without them, work does not get done and goals do not get accomplished. If goals do not get accomplished, then organizations do not experience success and it is only a matter of time before they cease to exist.

Plant managers oversee many employees in manufacturing facilities. These people perform a variety of different tasks, and they need to be motivated to perform at optimal leaves...especially if their jobs are repetitive and mundane. For this reason, motivational skills are important for plant managers.

Plant managers can motivate employees in a variety of different ways. One method involves the use of work-life balance. Work-life balance helps employees accomplish work-related goals while enjoying their lives outside of work. As their lives get busier and more hectic, workers begin to realize the importance of work-life balance. Time is limited, and different things need to take priority at different times in their lives. People know that they need to work to sustain a certain lifestyle...but they also need the necessary time to enjoy that lifestyle.

Plant managers need to understand that work-life balance benefits their workforce in many ways including:

Reduced stress

To understand the benefits offered here, it is best to first obtain a better understanding of the negative effects of stress in the workplace. These include:

- *Fatigue* - When stress is too much, it wears on employees. They look tired and feel exhausted. When they go to bed at night, they are kept awake thinking about the issues that are bothering them. In the morning, they wake up well short of refreshed and have to deal with another stressful day.

- *Anxiety* - Excessive stress causes employees to worry about issues. They fret over what might happen or what has already occurred. Worrying is often difficult to control, and sometimes it makes absolutely no sense...like when people agonize about things that might transpire. This worrying is not justified because potential issues are not certain, and they are beyond people's control. Heavy stress, however, brings worrying to the forefront, and it is can do a lot of unnecessary damage including the hindering of job performance.

- *Irritability* - One of the most common negative effects of heavy stress at work involves anger and hostility. When employees experience difficulties that they can't seem to overcome, their unpleasantness toward others is a natural side effect. This hostility can be directed at customers, suppliers, or employees...and it is rarely justified. In fact, most times this type of behavior is based solely on the fact that people are under a lot of pressure.

- *Deteriorating physical health* - Employees under large amounts of stress at work tend to be consumed with their jobs. They spend more and more time trying to overcome obstacles as the list of unresolved issues gets longer. In essence, they are now living to work, instead of working to live. This results in health issues such as weight loss and high blood pressure. If left unchecked, those problems can lead to much bigger concerns including malnutrition, heart disease...and possibly even death.

Reduced absenteeism

Employees whose jobs are dependent on others to complete their work know how difficult it can be when the employees they depend on are absent. Job tasks become more time consuming and difficult and sometimes cannot be completed.

Individual employees are not the only ones affected by absenteeism. It impacts the entire organization by making it less efficient. Employees are hired for a reason, especially in today's lean times, and their absence breaks a link in the organizational chain that is difficult to repair. In short, absenteeism is very important to organizations because the bottom line is negatively affected when employees are not at work.

Absenteeism improves when employees find work-life balance. They enjoy their lives more and want to show up for work. They also have a stronger desire to achieve the goals and objectives of the organization.

Reduced turnover

Turnover is the process of losing and replacing employees. It is a concern for many manufacturers because it adds cost to an employer's bottom line. Employees who leave an organization typically need to be replaced, and the replacements need to be trained. There is a cost to that training, and that cost becomes higher as turnover increases.

Another concern with turnover involves errors. During training, mistakes happen...and those mistakes can be very expensive. Experienced employees tend to make fewer mistakes, and this helps an organization function more efficiently.

Work-life balance reduces turnover by addressing the needs that employees have outside of work. Employers who show interest in the personal lives of their employees benefit because those employees choose to remain employed at the organization. Their experience is valuable, and the cost of replacing it negatively impacts the bottom line.

Increased morale

Employee morale is the outlook employees have about their workplace. It involves their thoughts about the work they perform and their job satisfaction. When employees' morale is lowered, their drive to achieve organizational goals decreases, and their job satisfaction diminishes.

Work-life balance programs improve employee morale by addressing their work-related and non-work-related needs. The end result is a win-win for the manufacturers and employees.

Increased productivity

Productivity increases when employees have work-life balance because they feel more committed to the goals of their employer. When people believe they are being treated fairly, they want to give back...and the best way to give back in a manufacturing facility is to become more productive.

Skilled plant managers clearly see that work-life balance because it is beneficial for employees and manufacturers. It produces happier and more productive employees while reducing absenteeism and turnover.

Another method of motivation involves the application of Theory Y developed by Douglas McGregor. McGregor came up with two opposite management views called Theory X (negative) and Theory Y (positive). Theory X represents the plant manager trusting only herself to do the right thing. Theory Y represents the plant manager trusting herself and her employees.

McGregor's general belief was that we should not have negative preconceived notions about human nature. Specifically, he thought plant managers who believed employees were lazy would make biased decisions, often counterproductive, based on that thinking (Theory X). Theory Y made positive assumptions about people, including the thinking that they would exercise self-direction and assume responsibility if committed to organizational objectives.

Four basic assumptions sum up the premise of each theory. Under Theory X, the following negative assumptions are made:

- *Employees dislike work and try to avoid it.*
- *Employees need to be coerced, controlled, or threatened for task accomplishment.*
- *Employees elude responsibility and always need direction from supervision.*
- *Employees are not ambitious and prefer job security over innovation.*

Under Theory Y, the following positive assumptions are made:

- *Employees like work and look forward to it.*
- *Employees are self-directed for task accomplishment.*
- *Employees look for responsibility and are autonomous.*
- *Employees are creative and seek out novel ways to accomplish goals and expand horizons.*

As can be seen by Theory Y, employees are motivated to perform their jobs to the best of their abilities when they are trusted. Plant managers need to have the skills necessary to motivate employees, and those who succeed realize trust is critical.

The third method of motivation that can be used by plant managers involves setting goals for employees. A theory about goal setting was developed by psychologist Edwin Locke, and it is one of the most widely known and respected theories in organizational psychology. Locke's work helped people understand motivation at work and job satisfaction, and it has been applied in a variety of different manufacturing situations. In short, Locke thought employees should set difficult and specific goals, and those goals would lead to higher work performance. This theory challenges the idea that employees should simply "do their best" since that type of thinking does not motivate people to perform optimally.

Using goal setting as a motivational tool requires discretion on the part of plant managers because it has some limitations. For example, if employee goals differ from that of the manufacturer, then the resulting conflict could cause their job performance to suffer. Additionally, employees can become so obsessed with meeting their goals that they resort to inappropriate or unethical behavior to accomplish them. Based on this, it is rather obvious that plant managers who experience success with goal setting truly are skilled.

Communication

In production settings, plant managers have to work with employees, department managers, and senior management. This requires a wealth of interpersonal interaction, and it also requires good communication skills. Good communication skills are natural for some people, but they are not so natural for others. However, regardless of the innate level, everyone's communication skills can be improved with knowledge. For plant managers, this knowledge is obtained by first understanding the basic types of organizational communication known as formal, informal, and grapevine as shown below.

Formal

Formal communication includes presentations, speeches, trade shows, conferences, labor negotiations, forums, and seminars. Formal communication often involves a planned protocol and structured management. The protocol includes guidelines and rules concerning the reason for the formality, and the structured management consists of leaders who assume facilitator roles.

Plant managers use formal communication to conduct activities that are important and need to be understood by the people involved. The subject matter varies depending on the need, but it can be related to specific people, departments, divisions, or organizations.

Formal communication drives business transactions in most organizations. Sales are completed, budgets are determined, changes are made, training is conducted, and deals are finalized. When people are in a structured environment, they are likely to stick to the subject matter and make decisions, regardless of those decisions being good or bad, that impact the overall health of their organizations.

Informal

Informal communication is not as structured as formal communication. It occurs in face-to-face conversations, text messages, phone calls, and emails as part of employee socialization within the workplace. It typically takes place when employees are not working in situations where there are planned protocols and rigid hierarchies...such as lunch and breaks. However, it can also take place in formal situations if conditions allow. For example, an employee might pass a personal note to another employee during a video presentation.

Intestinally, informal communication is sometimes used as a prelude to formal communication. For example, a plant manager might ask her salespeople what they think of a new product before holding a formal presentation with customers. She might also discuss manufacturing concerns with his production managers before sending them a letter detailing their rising labor costs. Regardless of the reason, informal communication plays a big role in helping organizations achieve goals and objectives.

Grapevine

The grapevine is a type of informal communication, but it differs because it is based on hearsay that might or might not be supported by facts. Much of the information exchanged during grapevine communication is gossip or rumors, so it can be very misleading and cause unnecessary problems including stress, anxiety, fear, and depression. If these problems occur, then productivity decreases as does organizational efficiency.

Interestingly, there are times when the grapevine is the best way for employees to hear news about their organization. Confidential information is exposed and spreads from employee to employee until it is no longer confidential. This information tips people off about what is going to happen in the future and allows them the opportunity to react beforehand. For example, if they know they are going to get laid off, then they can look for another job before the ax falls. However, the downside is that employees never know for sure if what they are hearing is true, so a reaction might be unnecessary or unjustified...and it can lead to problems that otherwise would not have occurred. In short, the grapevine is important for organizational communication, but it can easily do more harm than good.

Regardless of the type, communication that occurs in organizations is important for plant managers because it impacts the goals and objectives of those organizations and it dictates the exchange of information.

Plant managers must also understand the directional flow of communication. This flow is determined by the organization and the leadership within it, and it is critical to the way organizations conduct business because it dictates the kind of information released and the people who discuss it.

The four major directions of communication flow are top-to-bottom, bottom-to-top, horizontal, and combination. Each of these flows is discussed below.

Top-to-bottom

Top-to-bottom communication flows in a downward direction. It starts at the top of the organization, often the plant manager, and trickles down the hierarchy until it reaches the rank-and-file employees. Organizational goals are an example of top-to-bottom communication. They start with top leadership and work their way down to all other employees. This information must be transmitted to every worker because it impacts the success or failure of the organization...and it has to start with the highest-ranking members of the hierarchy.

Unfortunately, top-to-bottom communication can be ineffective. Think about the game where one person whispers a phrase to another and then that person whispers the same phrase to another individual...and so on. The phrase often changes because words are lost or added during the transition from one person to the next. Apply that same thinking to a manufacturer with multiple layers of management including the plant manager, production managers, supervisors, leaders, and production employees. Add to this the staff positions such as sales, quality assurance, human resources, and accounting, and it is rather easy to see how information can be distorted or confused.

In a nutshell, top-to-bottom communication is a good method for transferring information, but it does have potential shortcomings in terms of plant management.

Bottom-to-top

The flow of bottom-to-top communication is the exact opposite of top-to-bottom. It starts with the rank and file workers and flows upward to employees at the top of the hierarchy. An example involves a new lathe being installed in a tool and die shop. The employees who work on the lathe give feedback on the value and performance of the machine to their line leaders. Their line leaders pass this information to the production manager, and the production manager transfers it to the plant manager.

Bottom-to-top communication can be advantageous if people are honest. In reference to the lathe above, employees who operate the machine understand the most about its shortcomings. Their honesty will reach the plant manager, and he will decide on whether to keep it or send it back. However, dishonest feedback from lower levels can lead to problems. Employees might like the performance of the lathe, but they do not like that it eliminates work and takes away money from their paychecks. For this reason, they fabricate many reasons why it does not perform properly, hoping that the plant manager will send it back.

Horizontal

Horizontal communication flows sideways. It does not move upward or downward, and it typically occurs between employees of the same status. Two warehouse employees discussing the division of inventory is an example of this flow. They exchange information with each other rather than with their supervisor.

Horizontal communication is valuable because it eliminates the potential distortion of information as it moves up or down the hierarchical ladder. Decisions can also be made faster because there is no waiting for supervisor approval. However, a drawback to horizontal communication is that wrongful or improper decisions can be made without input from higher-level employees. For example, the warehouse employees mentioned above might spend hours counting individual salt and pepper packets for sandwich preparation because they are unaware that management does not inventory these items. They would have saved money, time, and effort if they had input from those higher up in the organization.

Plant managers must be aware that horizontal communication occurs in their organizations. They need to seize upon its benefits, but also pay attention to the problems that it can cause.

Combination

There are times when organizational communication flows in multiple directions. For example, a company might want data from an ongoing process for statistical reasons. The plant manager issues a directive on the data that he needs, and this information flows top-to-bottom until it reaches the employees involved in the process. Once the data is collected, it flows from bottom to top until it reaches the plant manager.

Horizontal communication also plays a role here because employees communicate with each other to make sure the data they collect is accurate and meets the requirements outlined in the directive.

While plant managers must understand the direction flow of communication, they also need to understand the ways that employees communicate with each other and outsiders. These ways are known as methods.

Methods are the ways that people in organizations choose to communicate. These methods can be broken down into many different sub-categories, but this breakdown can be extensive and confusing. For example, a speech is a form of verbal communication and so is a taped video of that speech, but they are not the same because the live event has a different atmosphere than the taped version. However, for this book, the three major sub-categories of methods are non-verbal, verbal, and written.

These sub-categories can be used by themselves or in combination. For example, a meeting for all plant managers in North American facilities takes place in a company's United States headquarters. However, senior leadership also wants plant managers from the European and Asian facilities to know what happened in the meeting, so they send these individuals emails with the major points of discussion. In this situation, verbal and written communication are used for the same meeting because this combination is the best way to transmit the information needed for the people involved.

The following is a breakdown of the three method sub-categories for better understanding:

Non-verbal

Plant managers might not realize it, but a sizeable portion of their communication with others is non-verbal. Eye movement, posture, body position, hairstyle, body art, clothing, facial expression, shoulder shrugs, and hand gestures are all examples of non-verbal communication used to transfer information to others.

Certain elements of speech also play a role in non-verbal communication. These elements make up what is known as paralanguage, and they include voice quality, speed, pitch, tone, and volume. Paralanguage is so important that plant managers even use it during written communication. For example, the use of capital letters in email effectively means the sender is yelling or trying to get the reader's attention.

Not surprisingly, plant managers' non-verbal communication has a major bearing on their organizations and the people within them. They communicate with coworkers, suppliers, customers, and others using a variety of different techniques that do not involve the spoken or written word. Something as simple as a handshake means has a meaning that is understood by the parties engaging in the activity. A handshake is quite common and typically friendly, but other employee actions are not as welcoming. Ignoring someone, for example, is a much more unfriendly type of behavior that does not involve the spoken or written word...but it still has meaning for the people involved. In short, non-verbal communication influences employees' perceptions of others and affects their relationships.

The following are types of non-verbal communication that occur regularly in organizations:

- *Symbols* - These are intentional gestures, movements, or motions by employees to send signals or signs to others. Waving, putting thumbs up, putting thumbs down, pointing, raising a fist, throwing hands up in the air, and using fingers to indicate a number are all examples of symbols used in organizations.

- *Facial expressions* - Facial expressions are a very common and important aspect of non-verbal communication because the face is the first thing people see. Typically, the face is seen before any words are spoken, and it indicates what is about to transpire. Laughing, crying, frowning, wincing, winking, and staring are all examples of facial expressions used in organizations.

- *Paralanguage* - As noted earlier in this section, some components of speech are part of non-verbal communication. These components are known as paralanguage, and they include voice quality, speed, pitch, tone, and volume. Paralanguage is common in organizations when employees want to emphasize their points or positions.

- *Body position* - Body position is employees' posture, stance, or pose while interacting with others. It can indicate a variety of feelings including anger, pride, embarrassment, guilt, defensiveness, and shame. Arm crossing, leg crossing, head lowering, head raising, slouching, and chest protrusion are examples of body language used in organizations.

- *Space position* - This is the amount of space employees keep between themselves and others. It is dictated by a variety of factors including situation, culture, social norms, and worker's personalities. Getting close to people, keeping a distance from people, and walking away from people are examples of space positions used in organizations.

- *Exterior presentation* - Exterior presentation essentially involves developing an image based on the way employees look, the items they wear, or the things they have on their bodies. Clothing, jewelry, tattoos, uniforms, hats, and hairstyle are examples of exterior presentation used in organizations.

- Interestingly, the intent of this non-verbal communication can go from one extreme to the other. Some employees want to personalize their appearance, while others want to show they are part of a group. Employees who display personal intent with their exterior presentation want to establish their identity as individuals in their organizations, while employees who display group intent with their exterior presentation want to establish their identity as part of their organizations.

- *Physical touch* - Also known as haptics, this occurs when employees touch each other during interaction. Similar to space position, it is also affected by a variety of factors including situation, culture, social norms, and people's personalities. Pats on the back, high-fives, and handshakes are all examples of physical touch used in organizations.

Verbal

This is likely the most well-known form of communication. It is a major constituent for every plant manager, and it consists of the spoken word. Organizations establish norms regarding verbal communication that are followed by all employees. Factors such as culture, age, workplace terminology, and industry-specific jargon influence the way employees speak to customers, suppliers, and coworkers.

Unlike written communication, verbal communication almost always takes place in real-time. However, verbal communication is similar to written communication because both can be conducted with multiple people involved. A conversation can involve a group of people, and a group of people can all write on the same document.

Verbal communication is sometimes misconstrued if employees cannot see each other because they miss out on non-verbal cues. Something as simple as raising one's eyebrows can send a signal that cannot be sent without being seen. However, verbal communication also has an advantage over non-verbal communication because it allows for faster absorption of information. Quite simply, people can speak and hear more words than they can write or read in the same amount of time.

Below are common ways in which verbal communication takes place in organizations.

- *Telephone* – Since telephones were added to workplaces and up until about 2005, they were the predominant form of organizational communication between people who were not meeting face-to-face. Since 2005, however, this standard has been replaced by a form of nonverbal communication known as email...even though telephone conversations are still quite common.

- *Face-to-face* – This is the oldest type of verbal communication known to humans. It takes place while employees are physically in the same place at the same time. They can look at each other while speaking, so non-verbal cues enhance the ability to actively listen.

- *Video conference* – Similar to face-to-face communication, video conferencing takes when employees talk to each other at the same time. However, video conferencing does not require employees to be physically in the same place, so it saves time and money in many organizational situations.

- *Radio and television* – Radio and television are sometimes classified as mass communication, but there is a verbal element involved. However, the speaker cannot hear the listener, and the listener cannot talk to the speaker. These deficiencies in the verbal communication process limit radio and television's effect on the participating employees, but they need to be mentioned.

Written

Plant managers must use written words in many different forms of communication including letters, memos, reports, instructions, legal documents, and signs. These words can be handwritten, typed, or professionally developed; and they can be composed using word processors, computers, email, texting, tweeting, or instant messaging. Regardless of the method used to display the wording, written communication transfers information to others.

Unlike verbal and non-verbal communication, written communication in organizations is often asynchronous. A plant manager usually does not write a document at the same time that the intended recipient is reading it. This asynchrony often prevents the immediate responses that can come during verbal and non-verbal communication, but it also allows documents to be perused in the future.

Written communication also allows for formality and permanence. Time can be taken to choose the exact wording necessary for complete understanding, and written documents are typically more binding than verbal expressions. Written communication is critical in business because, without it, many goals and objectives are not achievable. An example of this is the written certificate from an audit. Without this document, organizations might not be able to sell major customers; thereby preventing them from reaching sales goals and potentially creating financial instability.

Written communication is often standardized for an organization. "Standardized" refers to a specific way that documents are written. For example, company letterhead with a certain type, size, and color font might be required. Other organizations, specifically those in education, mandate specific writing styles such as APA (American Psychological Association) and MLA (Modern Language Association). Standardized documents are advantageous because they are easily identified; thereby preventing fraud and other illicit activity. However, learning the format can be cumbersome for employees and also change the focus from content to structure.

Regardless of whether or not written communication is standardized, there are specific sub-categories that are part of it. These sub-categories include letters, faxes, contracts, memos, reports, specifications, tweets, websites, email, text, and various forms of social media. Obviously, these sub-categories are important for virtually every organization...and that is why writing plays a major role in organizational communication.

Now you understand the type, direction, and methods people use to communicate in organizations. The following uses these three aspects of communication in one example for better understanding:

A plant manager issues a memo that dictates a $40 per month increase in the health insurance co-pay for all employees. First, the CEO meets with her vice presidents and gives them the memo explaining that rising health insurance costs are the reason for the increase. Then, the vice presidents meet with the branch managers and give each of these managers a copy of the memo. Finally, the branch managers meet with all of the employees at their specific branches.

In the above example, the type of communication is formal because it mandates a new rule for all employees. The direction of the communication flow is top-to-bottom because it starts with the

CEO and progresses down the organizational ladder until it reaches the rank-and-file employees. The method of communication is written because the information is transferred using a memo.

As most plant managers understand, communication in organizations does not always go as smoothly as in the above example. There are many roadblocks to the successful transmission of information, and that is why challenges need to be discussed

Plant managers also need to have the skills necessary to overcome barriers to effective communication. Communication barriers are roadblocks to understanding the meaning of messages sent from sender to receiver. In other words, they hinder communication between people.

Communication barriers cause a wealth of problems that decrease efficiency in manufacturing facilities. Misunderstanding prevents tasks from being accomplished; thereby hindering the achievement of organizational goals and objectives. When goals are not accomplished, manufacturers become stagnant...and some even cease to exist.

Workplace communication is influenced by a variety of different factors. Three major factors that need to be understood by plant managers include:

Noise

Many different kinds of noise create distractions in manufacturing workplaces. These distractions hinder communication by causing employees to misinterpret messages. Examples include telephones, faxes, production machinery, coworker conversations, customer visits, interviews, vendor appointments, audits, facility tours, music, and loudspeaker systems.

Hierarchy

Authority has a direct impact on communication in manufacturing facilities. Some employees high up on the corporate ladder do not make an effort to communicate with those on lower rungs. Interestingly, the opposite is also true. Some employees at lower levels do not try to communicate with those in higher positions. This makes absolutely no sense from an organizational communication standpoint, but it does happen quite frequently. These groups think of themselves as distinct, and they only communicate with coworkers on the same level.

Words

Certain words used in manufacturing workplaces are esoteric. This means they have meaning to people who possess specialized knowledge, but they are confusing to other individuals. For example, jargon results from words or expressions used in a particular trade, industry, or profession. They are very specific, and generally not understood by outsiders. An example is *trimmed to the blue* (a meat processing term that means all the fat has been removed from a ham during manufacturing).

Along the same lines as esoteric words, acronyms are abbreviations that represent specific words or phrases. FDA (Food and Drug Administration) is an example that is understood by a fairly wide variety of people. However, the majority of terms in this category are far less familiar...especially those from the military. Examples include NFO (Naval Flight Officer), DFAC (Dining Facility), and BCD (Bad Conduct Discharge).

Plant managers need the skill to break down and classify communication barriers for better understanding. The classification is as follows:

Selective perception

This involves employees who see and hear only what they want to see and hear. They do not consider any opposing, contradictory, or differing viewpoints because they have established a position where change is not an option. This is a barrier to communication because bias results when all viewpoints are not considered.

Emotional status

People interpret and send messages differently based on the emotions they are experiencing. For example, anger causes people to hear only what they want to hear, depression causes them to shut out others, fear causes them to analyze every word spoken, and nervousness causes them to lose focus of what is being said. Emotional status is a barrier to communication because it influences manufacturing employees' actions and reactions.

Filtering facts

This occurs when employees manipulate or change information so that it is received more favorably. For example, a worker who tells the plant manager that he rarely consumes alcohol would be filtering facts if he drinks every weekend. This is a barrier to communication because information is not being received accurately.

Information overload

This happens when people have too much information to process in their minds. Employees experiencing information overload essentially ignore information (they ignore all information and simply "walk away" from the matter), select information (they reject information that they designate as unimportant to pay closer to information that they designate as important), or forget information (they lose track of information and cannot remember what others have told them).

Information overload is a barrier to communication because people do not process all of the information they receive. This causes important aspects of discussions to be overlooked, ignored, or forgotten. Plant managers need the skill to overcome this barrier.

Language differences

As noted earlier, jargon and acronyms are examples of how words have different meanings to people. Language differences encompass jargon and acronyms...but they also include everyday words that are not specific to a trade, profession, or industry. For example, a young employee who says a new machine is "sick" means it is very cool, but a fifty-year-old employee views the word "sick" in a more negative light.

In short, language is not uniform, and confusion is possible when people think everyone shares a similar perception of the same words. Based on this, one can see that language differences present a barrier to communication for plant managers.

Nonverbal misunderstanding

Nonverbal communication is discussed in the politics section of this book, but it also deserves mention here because it involves actions other than words that lead to confusion. Two subdivisions of nonverbal misunderstanding include written words and nonverbal actions. The following examines each of these in more detail:

- *Written words*

  Written communication uses words in a variety of documents including letters, memos, reports, instructions, legal documents, and signs. The information can be handwritten, typed, or professionally developed, and it can be composed using word processors, computers, email, texting, tweeting, or instant messaging. Regardless of the method used to compose and display the wording, written communication transfers information to others in writing.

Written words are not understood and interpreted the same way by everyone. They are a barrier to communication because they can create misunderstanding in the workplace...and skilled plant managers are aware of this barrier.

- *Nonverbal actions*

  This involves virtually every aspect of nonverbal communication that is not written. Body movements, gestures, expressions, positions, and appearance are all part of non-verbal actions. Voice tone, pitch, and quality also fall into this category because they are not spoken words.

  People do not always see things the same way, and non-verbal actions can be interpreted differently based on individual perception. Plant managers need to realize that nonverbal actions present barriers to communication because they can create misunderstanding in the workplace.

Gender differences

Men and women have different perceptions of situations, and this can prevent them from effectively working together. Women tend to focus on indirect ways to resolve problems, and they rely on feelings for making decisions. Men often approach problem-solving in direct ways, and they rely on facts for decision-making. There is no "right" or "wrong" here, but plant managers need to be aware that gender differences can create problems in the workplace.

Cultural differences

Most people who have worked with cultures other than their own understand that the differences can create workplace challenges. These challenges are resolving themselves as organizations become global melting pots, but issues currently exist that negatively influence communication between employees. A good plant manager understands culture and takes action to prevent problems.

Withholding information

Some people intentionally remain silent to withhold information that other employees might find useful. This can cause a variety of workplace problems, and it is often done for job security or power reasons. Plant managers need to be able to extract withheld information so it can be put to use.

- Deceitful misrepresentation

This occurs when people purposely do not tell the truth. They manipulate facts, figures, or other information to benefit personally, and their actions cause problems in the workplace. Plant managers must be aware of employee deceit and work to discourage it.

The skill of communication is important for most jobs, but it is critical for plant managers due to the wide variety of people that they interact with on a daily basis. Astute plant managers believe the importance of good organizational communication cannot be overemphasized, so they make a continual effort to better it. Some suggestions to do so are listed below.

Encourage feedback

Company meetings regarding internal communication might not be realistically possible, but that does not prevent employee perceptions from being tapped. Plant managers should consider issuing annual surveys that give an idea of the communication climate. Additionally, a suggestion box also provides employees with the opportunity to improve communication problems. However, regardless of the method for getting information about communication, employees need to be assured that their survey responses and suggestions will be kept confidential.

Another way to encourage feedback is for plant managers to simply ask employees questions about their communication with others in their organizations. Employees perceive workplace experiences differently, and their input could trigger some ideas for making overall communication better. Additionally, those employees feel like they are being heard and their viewpoints are important.

When plant managers encourage feedback from employees, they are involving these employees in communication problems and resolutions to those problems. This promotes empowerment, and empowerment leads to happier and more productive workers.

Clarify wording

This improvement technique is specific to written communication. Sometimes plant managers can improve communication by simply wording written documents so they are more easily understood. If communication problems stem from a misunderstanding of what is written, then the document serves no purpose other than to confuse employees. Time and effort should be invested to assure comprehension of the material because workers who lack comprehension will pass on inaccurate information. Quite simply, if written documents are easily understood, then communication will improve.

Avoid unnecessary change

Smart plant managers understand that change is necessary for their organizations to grow and prosper. However, some changes are made for improvement while other changes are made simply to do so. An example is a plant manager who reorganizes the plant's management structure every year. This type of change does not make sense because employees are unsure about what they need to do to keep their new bosses happy. Communication breaks down within the entire organization until a learning curve is completed. Unfortunately, as soon as workers are aware of what is expected of them, another management restructuring occurs. In short, communication will improve if unnecessary changes are eliminated or, at the very least, minimalized.

Problem-solving

Problem-solving is an extension of decision-making, but it warrants a discussion of its own because it is a core component of a plant manager's job. Manufacturing facilities experience a wealth of problems, and that is why supervisors are needed in virtually every department. Those supervisors, however, are not all capable of resolving issues within their own jurisdiction, so they seek out the assistance of a higher-up individual known as the plant manager.

Problem-solving skills are an absolute must for plant managers because, without them, they cannot do their jobs effectively. They need to assess a wide variety of different problems and act accordingly...which is typically much easier said than done. To better understand the overall skill of problem-solving, it is best to break it down into the following sub-skills:

Investigation skills

Managers in every organization need investigation skills to resolve problems. However, plant managers must be able to quickly ascertain problems and resolve them at a moment's notice. In manufacturing facilities, factors such as production deadlines, sales promotion demands, machinery downtime, and product scheduling issues all make time management a critical aspect of the investigating process. Plant managers who cannot properly manage their time will find the investigation process much more difficult; thereby making it challenging to solve problems

Mechanical skills

Mechanical skills are important for problem-solving because manufacturing operations use production machinery to assemble products. These machines break down over time, and the pace is often fast and furious. However, broken machines are not a major issue if they can be fixed, so plant managers must understand what needs to be done to get those machines running properly in a reasonable amount of time. This saves manufacturers money, and it allows them to get their products to the customers who need them.

Project management skills

Project management is exactly what it says...it is the management of projects. To be properly managed, every project needs a plan of action... and plant managers are in charge of developing that plan.

An example of a project where a plant manager's skills are needed is a bakery. The objective of the bakery is to establish a new production line for pretzels. More specifically, this line must be able to manufacture 600 pretzels per hour or 4800 pretzels in an eight-hour shift. This objective needs to be kept in mind by the plant manager throughout the project to assure it is accomplished. For example, if an engineer determines that the line is only capable of producing 3200 pretzels in an eight-hour shift, then the plant is obligated to stop the project from moving forward until the necessary changes are made to meet productivity standards. The following are other factors that the plant manager must keep in mind:

- *Materials*

  Materials for the pretzel line project need to be managed, and this involves asking questions. What materials will be needed? Has everything been ordered? When will the materials arrive? Where will the materials be stored? All of these questions need to be answered for the project to flow smoothly. Plant managers might not do the actual ordering or inventorying of the materials, but they need to oversee the overall process.

- *People*

  People involved in the project need to be identified...regardless of whether they are company employees or contracted workers. Again, this involves asking questions. Who will be needed to complete the pretzel line project? When and where will they be needed? People involved in design, engineering, employee safety, food safety, quality assurance, and testing will all need to be part of the pretzel line, and their involvement needs to be managed. Plant managers need to tap the expertise of all of these individuals to keep the project moving forward. They do not need to do the actual work because the people are qualified to do their jobs, but those people need to be told when and where their services are needed.

- *Timeframe*

Some projects tend to go on forever, and this is usually due to poor management. Plant managers need to establish time frames for completion so people are aware of what they need to do and where they need to be in terms of accomplishing tasks. The time allotted for the pretzel line is 120 days from the start of the project. The required raw materials (ingredients, packaging, boxes, etc.) must be in the bakery 90 days after the project has started, and the test product must be run within 100 days. Based on these requirements, the product will be ready to hit the store shelves within the 120-day timeframe.

- *Cost*

Cost is a factor for most activities in organizations, and it needs to be a factor for the pretzel line. It has been determined that the total cost for the pretzel line must not exceed $200,000. This includes design, production equipment, installation, and testing. If the cost exceeds $200,000, then the plant manager is obligated to stop the project from moving forward until a decision to spend the extra money has been made. For example, the CEO of the bakery needs to sign off for the additional funding for the project to be approved.

- *Evaluation*

This is done after the pretzel line project has been completed. Did everything go as planned? Were there major problems? If so, what needs to be changed now and for similar projects in the future? The plant manager needs to make sure this does not turn into a "blame game" where people are singled out for problems or mistakes. The goal is to evaluate the project, make improvements, and note changes for the future.

Innovative skills

Product managers must understand that innovation adds value to manufacturing. This value can be internal or external, and it is often complex because it cannot always be defined by a single event. For example, product development often involves testing different prototypes in different markets to find where there is consumer demand. If a new product is scrapped because it did not work in the first market it was tested in, then there is no innovation...there is only an idea. In short, plant managers need the ability to come up with new ideas or improve concepts that already exist.

Some people think that innovation is only important for technology-based companies. While it is critical for these types of businesses, it also has significance for manufacturing. No manufacturer wants to become obsolete, and to avoid this they need to be innovative.

Some of the benefits offered by innovation include:

- *Increased productivity*

  Innovation drives people to work harder, and that is why innovative manufacturing facilities have more productive employees. Manufacturers that are constantly looking to implement ideas and concepts need more from their employees, and those employees rise to the occasion when they are allowed to be innovative.

- *Increased motivation*

  The explanation for this benefit is fairly simple and straightforward. People are inspired to work for innovative manufacturers because they like being involved in projects that are new or different.

Novel ideas and concepts are constantly being put into action, and this motivates employees to do their jobs to the best of their ability.

- *Increased creativity*

  Creativity fuels innovation, but that creativity is wasted if it is not put into action. Innovative manufacturers have people on staff who are qualified to ensure ideas are put into action. This does not guarantee success, but it assures creators that their ideas will be taken to the next level.

  In short, employees that work for innovative manufacturers are more likely to be creative because they know their ideas will be followed through. This gets creative juices flowing and opens doors to new ways of thinking.

- *Increased competitiveness*

  Consumers purchase products to make their lives easier. The internet has made them more informed than they ever were in the past and it also gives them a variety of options. Innovation gives manufacturers an advantage because it keeps them on the cutting edge and ahead of the competition.

Report writing

Most people who have written a report for school understand that it can be a tedious and difficult task. Research has to be conducted, facts need to be discovered, and information needs to be well written and accurate. In business, reports also require research that includes uncovering the facts. They are written for a variety of reasons including injury, theft, accidents, damage, harassment, intimidation, discrimination, and other incidents that occur in workplaces. These reports need to contain all pertinent information, but they are often written with inaccuracies. Common errors include those listed below.

- Facts are missing or inaccurate.
- Times and dates are missing or inaccurate.
- People who are involved are not interviewed.
- Interviews are not in-depth.
- Interviewers do not ask the right questions.

The above list is not complete, but it does show how report writing can be inaccurate. If this is the case, then wrong conclusions can be drawn and decisions regarding those conclusions can be unjust. Plant managers need to know how to write detailed investigative reports that have measures in place to prevent facts and information from being inaccurately entered or omitted.

Based on the legal aspects involved with workplaces today, the content of the reporting has become much more detailed than it ever was in the past. Plant managers must consider all related factors while documenting detailed facts about the allegation. Information is typically gathered qualitatively and it is used to make a quantitative analysis. For example, in the case of sexual harassment, the plant manager needs to interview (or designate someone to interview) the accuser, accused, witnesses, and anyone else who knows something about the alleged incident. In terms of interviewing, more is better because common denominators and general consensus can be extracted. This process of interviewing large numbers of people is known as qualitative information gathering. That information is then analyzed and a conclusion is drawn. In the case of sexual harassment, the conclusion is a decision that determines whether the accused is guilty or not guilty of the accusation. This decision-making process is quantitative because it provides an exact answer.

Below is an example of how business investigative reports should be written by plant managers or their designated employees. Each section is shown beginning with the Executive Summary.

Executive Summary

A discussion on the executive summary is somewhat premature at this point, but it is important to understand what it is and why it exists. Quite simply, an executive summary provides an image of the incident that took place for everyone that needs to know what happened. It is typically placed at the beginning of the report, but it is not written until the report is finished.

An executive summary is very important. In fact, it is sometimes the most important aspect of an investigative report because readers make decisions to stop or continue reading based on it. In short, it provides a snapshot of the alleged behavior or wrongdoing, the investigation of that alleged behavior or wrongdoing, and the outcome of that investigation. If done correctly, an investigative summary is all the reader needs to obtain a basic understanding of the report and its findings.

Example

On November 23, 2018, Andover Industries received a complaint from a wheelchair-confined handicapped worker, Bob Mills, who claimed he was being harassed. Specifically, Bob said that Nick Williams called him "retard" and "Mr. Efficient" causing him to become embarrassed, angry, demotivated, and non-productive.

On November 24, 2018, I, Ralph Johnson, interviewed Mr. Mills and three different witnesses who supported his claims. Mathew Houghton, Trish Danielson, and Lyn Presnal all stated that this harassment has been ongoing for the past few months.

I interviewed Mr. Williams on November 26, 2018, and he admitted he had made "a few comments" over the past week, but he denied making these comments for the past three months. He also stated that his comments were made jokingly and everyone viewed them as "light-hearted humor."

Based on my interviews, I substantiate Mr. Mills' claim of harassment. I recommend Mr. Williams be required to undergo the diversity acceptance training offered by our human resources department. I also informed Mr. Williams that a copy of this written report would be available for him by November 29, 2018.

The section following the Executive summary is known as the Opening.

Opening

Essentially, the opening section encapsulates important information regarding the investigation concisely in terms that everyone can understand. The introduction to the Andover Industries' report is as follows:

Complaint identifier - CC441-10

Date of complaint - November 23, 2018

Accuser - Bob Mills

Accuser work information

Hire date – June 17, 2006
Position - Sander
Department – Finishing
Plant – Holman Technology
Supervisor – Roscoe Tillman
ID – 2113P

Accuser personal information

Address –
21455 Alexander St.
Avon Lake, OH 44012
DOB – 9/12/81
Phone - 216-221-4725
Work phone – Not applicable
Email - bob.mills@gmail.com
Work email – Not applicable
Social media – NA
Spouse – Erica Mills

Accused - Nick Williams

Accused work information

Hire date – October 22, 2015
Position - Grinder
Department – Finishing
Plant – Holman Technology
Supervisor – Roscoe Tillman
ID – 4229P

Accused personal information

Address –
29001 Redstone Court
Apt. 211
Cleveland, OH 44015
DOB – 8/17/93

Phone - 216-515--3756
Work phone – Not applicable
Email - nickwill93@hotmail.com
Work email – Not applicable
Social media –
Twitter - @nickwill93
Facebook - Nick Williams
Spouse – Not applicable

Investigator

Ralph Johnson
Plant Manager
Holman Technology
3400 Richdale Rd.
Cleveland, OH 44109
Work Email - ralph.johnson@andover.com
Work phone - 216-774-2300 X - 3775

The opening provides some details that are not listed anywhere else in the investigative report. It provides information about the accuser, accused, and investigator for a basic understanding before moving into the rest of the report.

The next section is known as the incident, and it provides some specifics about the accusation and situation.

Incident

This is the section where the investigator describes what happened. The incident to the Andover Industries' report is as follows:

What is the accusation?

The accuser (an employee) alleges workplace harassment by the accused (a coworker).

Who is the accuser? Bob Mills

Who supervises the accuser? Roscoe Tillman

Who is accused? Nick Williams

Who supervises the accused? Roscoe Tillman

What are the specifics of the accusation?

In reference to the Andover Industries' report, the incident is as follows:

Bob Mills, a sander in the finishing department at the Holman plant, alleges that Nick Williams, a grinder in the finishing department at the Holman plant, has called him derogatory names on several occasions. Bob says that he put up with the harassment until it became unbearable; thereby affecting him psychologically and causing him to lose focus on his job responsibilities.

Now it is time to narrow the focus of the investigation, and this is done in the scope section.

Scope

This section of the report lists all the steps in the investigation. The scope for the Andover Industries' report is as follows:

This investigation focuses on a complaint filed by one employee against another employee. The alleged victim, alleged accuser, and three witnesses are interviewed to obtain details on the situation. Those details will be used to piece together what really happened and determine if the alleged complaint is legitimate.

Now we can move into the interviews section. This is where most of the important information for the report is obtained.

Interviews

This section discusses every interview taken during the investigation. It essentially asks those involved to share their versions of the situation by discussing people involved, happenings, dates, times, statements, conversations, and behaviors. It is the most detailed section in the report, and it is useful for scrutiny or challenges that might arise later on.

The interviews for the Andover Industries' report were conducted in person by Ralph Johnson, Human Resource Manager at Holman Technology. Ralph asked the interviewees to provide their name, job, employee ID, and length of employment along with a detailed description of what happened on November 23, 2018.

On November 24, 2018, five employees were interviewed including Bob Mills, Nick Williams, Mathew Houghton, Trish Danielson, Lyn Presnal, and Roscoe Tillman. Please note the following regarding these interviews:

- All interviews were voluntary.
- All interviews took less than ten minutes to complete.
- All statements provided were signed by the interviewees.
- None of the employees had to be re-interviewed.

The interviews are listed below.

Bob Mills (accuser)

I am Bob Mills, employee ID 2113P, and I work for Andover Industries as a Sander in the finishing department at the Holman plant. I have worked for Andover Industries for 12 years including 5 years at the Saddle Design and 7 years at Holman Technology.

On November 23, 2018, at about 1:00 pm, Nick William made fun of me by calling me a "retard" because I am confined to a wheelchair and need help maneuvering when performing my job duties. Specifically, another employee needs to operate a lift when I need to sand machinery at levels that I cannot reach from the ground. I was offended by this and told nick that I am very capable of doing my job to the satisfaction of my boss, Roscoe Tillman, but all he did was grin and say "you are right, so I will call you Mr. Efficient."

Nick has made fun of me in the past, but this time I was very upset and decided to file a harassment complaint with human resources at the Holman plant. I filed the complaint because I was so mad that I could not focus on my job responsibilities and believed something needed to be done to stop Nick from insulting me.

Nick Williams (accused)

I am Nick Williams, employee ID 4229P, and I am employed at the Andover Industries' Holman Technology plant as a Finisher in the Finishing Department. I have worked for Andover Industries for 3 years at the Holman plant.

On November 23, 2018, at about 1:00 pm, I made fun of Bob by calling him "retarded," and he went to HR to complain about my comment. The fact of this matter is that I was completely joking, and Bob knew I was joking. We kid back and forth all the time, so I don't know why this time is such a big deal. He has said stuff to me in the past, but I have never filed a complaint. This situation has been blown way out of proportion by Bob and everyone else. This company is way too sensitive about kidding around and, in this situation, a "mountain is being made out of a molehill."

Mathew Houghton (witness)

I am Matt Houghton, employee ID 2006P, and I work for Andover Industries as a Sander in the Finishing Department at the Holman plant. I have worked for Andover Industries for 14 years at Holman Technology.

On November 23, 2018, at about 1:05 pm I witnessed Nick Williams call Bob Mills a "retard." Bob became upset and said something to Nick that I could not hear. He then looked even angrier and said he was going to Human Resources to file a complaint.

Trish Danielson (witness)

I am Trish Danielson, employee ID 9225L, and I work for Andover Industries as Inventory Control Specialist in the Inventory Department at the Holman plant. I have worked for Andover Industries for 4 years at Holman Technology.

On November 23, 2018, at about 1:00 pm I heard Nick Williams call Bob mills a "retard," causing Bob to get mad. Bob told Nick he did not want to be called names and abruptly walked away. I did not know where Bob was going, but he was moving quickly. After Bob left, Nick thought the situation was funny.

Lyn Presnal (witness)

I am Lyn Presnal, employee ID 9811Q, and I work for Andover Industries as a Quality Assurance Technician in the Quality Department at the Holman plant. I have worked for Andover Industries for 2 years at Holman Technology.

On November 23, 2018, at about 1:00 pm I witnessed Nick Williams call Bob mills a "retard." I did not hear Bob's response, but he said something back to Nick while Nick laughed at him. Bob then said he was going to human resources and stormed off.

Roscoe Tillman (supervisor of accused and accuser)

I am Roscoe Tillman, employee ID 1744P, and I am employed at the Andover Industries' Holman Technology plant as the Finishing Supervisor in the Finishing Department. I have worked for Andover Industries for 28 years including 6 years at the Prevention Controls facility and 22 years at Holman Technology.

I did not witness the situation between Bob Mills and Nick Williams, but Bob told me in the past control many different aspects of work including productivity, performance, and quality. However, plant managers need to realize that these policies and procedures often have little to do with political correctness. Instead, political correctness is mostly driven by unwritten rules. Employees conform because they believe it is the right thing to do...not because they are forced to do so. For example, documented policies state that sexual harassment is not tolerated, and any form of it is illegal and punishable by suspension or termination. However, "tattling" on employees is not prohibited by written policies and procedures. There is no formal punishment for "tattling," but it is often regarded as politically incorrect behavior. Employees who are thought of as tattlers are ignored or shunned in many instances because they violated a cultural norm.

Another example of culture involves using "we" instead of "I." It is not always politically correct to say "I finished the job." Instead, "we finished the job" is much better because it gives credit to others. This thinking is gaining popularity in organizations due to the increasing reliance on teams to solve problems. Plant managers must be aware that team members all have unique strengths that add diversity, and their differing viewpoints contribute to overall effectiveness. In areas where some members are weak, others are strong...and their combined efforts work together to solve problems. The synergy improves decision-making and helps teams reach goals within limited time frames. In many companies, selfishness is thought of as improper, and sharing is the cultural norm. The old saying, "there's no I in TEAM" has a place in a growing number of manufacturers...and plant managers are a major influence on its existence.

The last example of culture and political correctness involves socializing. Some cultures frown on employee socializing while others encourage it. Plant managers need to understand that "employee socialization" is typically not going to be found in a written policy or procedure, but there are unofficial expectations. Employees who socialize above expected norms risk furthering their careers in their organizations. Along the same lines, employees who refuse to socialize might be thought of as outcasts; thereby jeopardizing their chances for advancement or rewards.

Human resource management

Human resource management (HRM) is all about the management of people and workplace cultures. It uses strategies designed to meet management objectives by maximizing employee performance. These strategies incorporate the goals of organizational leaders while adhering to government laws, rules established by collective bargaining agreements, and other regulatory requirements.

Human resource management (HRM) is more important for plant managers now than it ever has been in the past. People are typically in place to run human resource departments within manufacturing facilities, but plant managers need to be involved to get the most out of those people and benefit from the result of their efforts. Below are some of the main reasons why HRM is important for plant managers and why they need to be involved.

Recruitment

that he would prefer not to work with Nick. When I asked him why he did not want to work with Nick, he said it was due to "personality differences" that did not involve the job. I tried to separate Bob and Nick as much as possible, but they work in the same department, sometimes on the same jobs, so keeping them apart all the time is not practical.

Now that the problem has been defined and the witnesses' accounts of what transpired have been documented, it is time to move forward. The next section analyses the information available so a decision can be made about the innocence or guilt of Nick Williams.

Analysis

I, Ralph Johnson, conducted the entire analysis.

I found that all three of the witnesses' stories corroborated; thereby determining that their stories must all be accurate. This finding of accuracy is further supported by the fact that all three witnesses have never been written up or disciplined for anything while employed at Andover Industries. In short, they are employees in good standing with the company.

I also believe that there have been problems between Bob Mills and Nick Williams based on my interview with their supervisor, Roscoe Tillman. He tried to keep these two apart, but their separation is not in the best interest of Andover Industries, so his decision to have them work together in certain instances is justified. Roscoe only has one write-up during his employment at Andover, and that was for attendance issues in 1994, so his testimony is further supported due to his good standing with the company.

The only story I found to be false is that of Nick Williams because he was the only person with this version of the story. Nick does not believe his behavior was offensive or abusive, but he is clearly wrong based on the no harassment policy that Andover Industries has had in place since 1995. Nick Williams has two previous write-ups documented on his record in the 3 years that he has worked here. He unsuccessfully argued that he was not guilty in both instances; thereby raising questions about his truthfulness in this situation.

Conclusion

Based on my analysis, I find that Bob Mills' allegation that Nick Williams harassed him is true. Mr. Williams' behavior fits the definition of harassment as defined in the Anderson Industries' employee handbook, and there is no "grey" area that warrants discussion.

This report and its findings will be passed to Henrietta Kowalski, Director of Human Resources for Anderson Industries, and she will decide what type of disciplinary action, if any, will be taken against Nick Williams.

Recommendations

The findings of this investigation show that harassment exists in the workplace at Anderson Industries. We should benefit from this incident by incorporating measures that will help prevent harassment in the future. I recommend mandatory diversity training for all employees at least once per year. This training will highlight the differences between employees and offer ways to help our workers accept those differences. Additionally, question and answer sessions should be available for employees who are unsure of what is expected of them in terms of diversity acceptance.

Review

Regardless of how good your report might be, it is critical to review it before submitting it to others. The following should be considered:

- Were any pertinent facts left out? Is anything missing? Were all "rocks uncovered?"
- Were all witnesses interviewed? Did anyone else see what happened? If so, can they be located and interviewed?
- Is the conclusion bias? Is the investigative report writer honest and sincere? Is there any type of discrimination?
- Were all relevant factors taken into account? Did the accuser have a reason to go after the accused? Was the accused targeted?
- Were the circumstances taken into account? Did the accused have mental health problems,

excessive stress, physical illness, or something else that caused them to do what they did?

- Are there any spelling or grammatical errors? Do these errors make the writer look careless? Should the report be edited by a professional?
- Does the report need to be reviewed by attorneys? Is the report safe from a legal standpoint? Is it possible that a lawsuit could result?
- Is the report stored in a secure place? Is it only assessable to authorized people? Can unauthorized people view it?

All of the above questions need to be considered by an astute plant manager to write a well-written, unbiased, and accurate report. A thorough review could prevent mistakes that end up leading to other problems...including legal action.

Delegation

Most plant managers need to delegate tasks to achieve the goals that have been set by themselves or their organizations. Delegation is essential for plant managers because they cannot accomplish everything they need to do without the help of others. When they delegate, they relieve some of their workload, and this allows them to focus on other tasks. They must assign responsibilities to subordinate employees....or they jeopardize their own jobs due to performance issues.

Plant managers need to understand that productivity increases when work is delegated. This is because that work can be broken down into manageable portions and given to different employees. Psychologically, this is easier on employees than handling an entire project because they are not faced with an overwhelming amount of work that needs to be finished. They see a small of work, and this inspires them to get it done. In this sense, delegation empowers workers because they are given a job and have decision-making power. They then take responsibility for the jobs they are performing, and that responsibility commits them to the goals and objectives of the organization.

Delegation is beneficial because it gives employees the opportunity to learn. They are assigned specific tasks, and they are responsible for following those tasks through to completion. This takes time and effort, but it also provides a real-world learning experience that cannot be obtained by reading a book or sitting in a classroom. Smart plant managers understand this education is valuable, and that is one reason why they delegate.

Plant managers also need to understand that manufacturing facilities operate more efficiently when work is delegated because jobs can be matched with employees' skills. This allows for the jobs to be broken down based on expertise. For example, cost aspects can be delegated to accountants, specification aspects can be delegated to quality assurance people, architectural aspects can be delegated to engineers, and training aspects can be delegated to human resources personnel.

When plant managers cannot delegate, they often end up micromanaging. This means they devote major time to minor details and focus intently on aspects of their jobs that they consider important. Unfortunately for their subordinates, this means every detail of their job is scrutinized...which often hinders productivity.

The actions of micromanaging plant managers are not all bad. In fact, their decisions are usually well thought since they are typically capable individuals who understand the needs of the manufacturing facility. However, the downside of their actions is their counter-productivity. Many times their subordinates are perfectly capable of making decisions, but they are not allowed to do so by micromanaging plant managers. This delays tasks from getting completed, hinders organizational efficiency, and prevents goals and objectives from being accomplished.

Plant managers who micromanage also prevent mistakes by making sure their employees adhere to specific details of work-related tasks. However, for the most part, micromanagers hinder productivity by monitoring processes and procedures far too closely. They are sometimes known as "workplace bullies" due to the high level of control that they possess...and their refusal or inability to delegate or relinquish that control.

Based on the above, it is rather obvious delegation is useful in organizations. However, plant managers also need to understand that there are times when they should not delegate work. For example, they should not delegate work simply because it is something that they do not enjoy doing. If plant managers have important tasks that they need to attend to and their plate is full, then they should delegate menial work to their subordinates. However, if they delegate work simply because they do not want to do it, then that is a clear sign of laziness…and plant employees will see this as a weakness.

Plant managers also need to keep their power in check so they do not abuse it. In terms of delegation, this means that they cannot believe their power gives them the right to delegate everything to others. While this might actually be true in some cases, it is not right…and it counteracts many of the benefits of delegation.

One last situation where work should not be delegated is when employees do not have the expertise to handle it. If these individuals are not capable, then they will not get the job done. Plant managers who ignore this rule will end up causing problems for their employees and their facility.

One way that plant managers can avoid delegation problems in their facilities is to follow a few basic guidelines. These guidelines include:

Matching expertise

It is important to select the right employee for the job. Employees are easily discouraged when they do not have the expertise to handle a task that has been delegated to them. Every plant manager can delegate, but choosing the person with the right skills for the task is much more difficult. In terms of matching expertise, "failing to plan, means planning to fail."

Explaining reasoning

Employees need to be made aware of the reason for the delegation. Workers want to know why there are performing a task and what their contribution means...rather than simply being told to do it. When they understand the reasoning, they take ownership of the task, and this increases the chance for success. Plant managers need to understand that employees who do not know why they are doing something feel like mushrooms...they are left alone to grow in the dark!

Define responsibilities

Employees need to know exactly what is expected of them. Plant managers who fail to define responsibilities do much more damage to their organizations than they realize. Valuable resources are depleted when employees are not sure of their responsibilities. Time, effort, and money are wasted until they understand exactly what is expected of them.

Encourage participation

Employees need to be involved in the process and asked for their opinions. This motivates them to take action and inspires them to do their best. Plant managers who do not encourage feedback lose out on valuable information that could be provided by the employees doing the work. That information could be used to make the completion of future tasks faster and more efficient.

Follow-up

Plant managers need to communicate with employees after they have been delegated tasks. Lines of communication should be kept open for questions and comments. Follow-up is about being proactive rather than reactive. Plant managers who do not establish a dialog with their employees are not available to answer questions that arise, and the end result is workers getting off track.

Provide feedback

Plant managers need to let employees know how they performed after their tasks are completed. After all, these employees invested a lot of time and effort, and they deserve to hear about the outcome. Additionally, compliments and constructive criticism help build relationships that assure success with the next delegated task. Plant managers who do not provide feedback are making a mistake because feedback drives the change that is necessary for making improvements in the future.

Negotiation

Negotiation is a process where people settle their differences by reaching an agreement. The goal is to reach that agreement with compromise from both sides. There will be some disagreement, but arguing should be minimal with the focus being on principle rather than position.

Negotiation is important for plant managers because conflicts arise due to different viewpoints, wants, and needs. Without it, people would argue to no end, dislike each other, and be dissatisfied. Negotiation allows people to reach agreements that satisfy everyone involved. This does not mean that people will get exactly what they want. It means that they will get some things they want while compromising on others. If done correctly, negotiation creates a win-win situation.

Win-win situations are almost always better than win-lose situations, but it must also be remembered that the goal of each party is to negotiate an outcome that is best for their interests. This thinking can be applied to negotiation in organizations. For example, a union wants what is best for its members while management wants what is best for the company.

Negotiation occurs in organizations for a variety of reasons. When conflicts arise, they need to be resolved...and negotiation is the best process to achieve that resolution. Without some type of negotiation process, warring factions never cease. This negatively impacts workplaces in terms of growth and prosperity, and it can lead to an organization's demise. Astute plant managers understand the importance of negotiation, and they take it very seriously. They also make sure that the people doing their negotiating have the necessary skills to get the job done.

Negotiation skills evolve from many different factors. All of these factors cannot be discussed in the scope of this book, but some of the major ones for plant managers are listed below.

Planning

This might be the most important factor because planning prepares plant managers for the entire negotiating process. Well planned negotiations have a much better chance of being successful than poorly planned negotiations.

Planning involves:

- *Determining goals and objectives* - Know your objectives and the other party's objectives. Think about ideal outcomes, acceptable outcomes, and unacceptable outcomes to the negotiation.

- *Conducting research* - Learn as much as possible about the other party. Try to figure out what techniques and ideas can be used to influence their thinking. Also, try to find similar negotiations and examine the outcomes for possible relationships.

- *Defining information limitations* - Determine the information that can be revealed to the other party and the information that needs to be kept confidential. This is important because some information can be used by the other party to strengthen their leverage in the negotiation process.

- *Preparing an agenda* - Decide the order in which issues need to be discussed. Sometimes the least significant concerns are discussed first to lead up to the more important ones, and other times the opposite occurs so the most important issues are discussed first. The order depends on the agenda...and that is why the agenda needs to be planned.

Assuming

Plant managers should never assume something is fact. In other words, avoid any type of bias during the negotiation. Try to find out exactly what the other party is looking for in the outcome. For example, a plant manager might assume that a union is trying to negotiate higher wages for its members when the union's actual goal is to prevent a loss of benefits.

Asking

Plant managers should avoid aggressive statements, ask open-ended questions, and focus on the other party's interests. Examples of these are as follows:

Aggressive vs. non-aggressive

Incorrect: This does not benefit the company in any way.
Correct: How is this beneficial to the company?

Closed-ended vs. open-ended

Incorrect: Are wages the union's major concern?
Correct: What are the union's major concerns?

Focus on one's own party vs. focus on the other party

Incorrect: The proposed health insurance plan is good for the company because we save money.
Correct: The proposed health insurance plan is good for the union because you have more options.

Understanding

Identify the reason for the negotiation, isolate the problems involved, and pinpoint areas for compromise. Plant managers who fail to understand these aspects of negotiation waste time and frustrate the other party.

Listening

Unfortunately, many people would rather hear themselves speak than listen to others. During negotiations, plant managers who are speaking cannot listen to what is being said by the other party....and they miss hearing important information that could be used to reach a compromise.

Listening is a learned skill that is often more important than speaking during negotiation. Maybe this is why people are born with two ears and only one mouth!

Observing

Similar to listening, observation is an important skill for plant managers. Watch the other party's gestures and reactions to determine if they are nervous, excited, or upset. Non-verbal communication provides a wealth of information that can be used to reach a compromise.

Actions often speak louder than words. It's simply a matter of interpreting those actions.

Communicating

Communication is necessary for preventing misunderstanding. Plant managers must convey their desired goals and the reasons why those goals are justifiable, and this is done through effective communication with the other party. Without effective communication, negotiations become confusing and frustrating...and compromises sometimes fail to be reached.

Controlling

This refers to controlling emotions. Plant managers need to control their emotions during negotiations or they risk failing to achieve their objectives. Unfortunately, this is not always easy to do because negotiations can bring out frustration, irritation, anger, happiness, relief, joy, and many other feelings related to emotions...especially if the discussion gets personal.

It is always best to keep emotions in check during negotiations. While this can be difficult, it is possible. Sometimes all it takes is the practice that comes with experience.

Deciding

People need to be able to make decisions during negotiations. Wishy-washy plant managers waste valuable time and often upset the other party in the process. This skill is especially important for compromising because opportunities arise instantaneously...and they disappear just as quickly.

One good thing about decision-making is the fact that it gets better with experience. Being involved in this aspect of a negotiation pays dividends the next time around.

Plant managers also need to use tactics to achieve the goals of their organizations. The following are some effective tactics that are very useful for negotiating purposes:

Offering

This tactic involves making the first offer. It's very difficult to determine which party should make the first offer in a negotiation. However, one rule to follow is to never make the first offer without knowing the real value of the subject being negotiated. For example:

Plant managers know that the average wage in their industry is $15 per hour, so they make the first offer of $13.50 per hour. This makes sense because they know where they want the wages to end up. They know the situation and their tactic of making the first offer is justified.

Bartering

This tactic involves trading one incentive for another to reach an agreement. For example:

A plant manager is negotiating a new contract with the union. The plant only needs 11 millwrights based on production volume, but the union wants to maintain the jobs of the current 15 millwrights. The plant manager agrees to keep the 15 jobs open in exchange for the union allowing the millwrights' wages to be frozen for the next three years.

In this case, the tactic of bartering was successful because each party believed they accomplished their goals.

Waiting

This tactic involves patience. Specifically, it refers to plant managers waiting before responding to an offer. It uses time to show that (1) there is no urgency and (2) other options are available. It also keeps the other side wondering if they offered enough incentive to reach an agreement.

Sectioning

Some negotiations fall apart because one or both of the parties refuse to compromise. They take an "all or nothing" approach and fail to reach an agreement. When this happens, both parties walk away unhappy.

A tactic used to deal with an "all or nothing" situation involves breaking the negotiations into smaller sections and dealing with each section on an individual basis. For example:

> A plant manager at a food processing company is in contract negotiations with the union representing truck drivers. One of the issues is that the union does not want drivers to work on Sundays because they need time to be with their families. However, the plant manager needs drivers to work on Sunday because products need to reach the stores daily.

> Both parties are unwilling to budge on this issue, so they decide to separately work on another area of the contract. They discuss the wage and benefit packages for the drivers and reach an agreement that out-of-pocket insurance costs will not rise for the next two years and wages will be limited to a three percent increase. This agreement does not resolve the Sunday work

issue, but it completes the wage and benefit part of the contract negotiation.

In this case, the tactic of sectioning allowed the parties to reach an agreement on a certain aspect of the negotiation, and it helps everyone feel like some progress was being made toward a resolution.

Prioritizing

This tactic establishes important aspects of the negotiation process including:

- *Separating business from personal*

    This expands upon the controlling factor discussed in the skills section. Plant managers need to focus on facts rather than their emotions. Emotional reactions can be very strong and work against the goals and objectives trying to be achieved. This is why business facts need to be prioritized over personal feelings during negotiations.

- *Determining issue significance*

    Issues are sometimes placed in order of importance to establish agendas that have the best chance of achieving goals and objectives. This allows plant managers to give more attention to top priorities in the beginning. For example:

Hourly wages are the most important concern for union workers, so they are discussed first and foremost during contract negotiations. Issues related to health care and paid holidays take a back seat until the wages aspect is resolved.

Taking the reins

This involves plant managers taking control of the agenda for the negotiations. Location, size of the room, time limits, and the number of negotiators all fall into this category. Some of these factors might not seem significant, but they can play an important role. It's comparable to a home-field advantage for a sports team.

Questioning

This expands upon the asking factor discussed in the skills section. Plant managers should ask questions rather than make concrete statements that result in arguments. For example:

Incorrect: Your offer is completely useless to the company.
Correct: Can you tell me how your offer benefits the company?

Incorrect: This will work well for the union.
Correct: Will this work well for the union?

Incorrect: The union does not understand the company's offer.
Correct: Would you like me to clarify the company's offer?

Always remember that questions open people up for discussion, and concrete statements shut them down.

Walking

This tactic is used by plant managers when the negotiation process fails and an agreement cannot be reached. Typically a future meeting is scheduled for further negotiation. This allows both sides to rethink their position and come back to the table with a new or different perspective.

The walking tactic should be a last resort. However, it works well to prevent:

- Heated arguments that result when negotiators disagree
- Wasted time that results when negotiators disagree
- Damaged working relationships that result when negotiators disagree

The above tactics are beneficial for reaching agreements, but plant managers still make common mistakes that hinder the development of agreements and compromises. These mistakes include those listed below.

Failing to plan

Plans need to be in place to properly reach an agreement. These plans should account for everything that might happen. While this might appear to be a daunting task, it is doable.

Many plant managers forget about or ignore the following factors that need to be a part of planning:

- *Research*

  Research compares similar cases for contrast and comparison purposes. Smart plant managers think about the following question regarding research:

  What were some similar union negotiations, what were the outcomes, and how do they relate to this negotiation?

- *Agenda*

  Agenda determines the basic strategy of the meeting. Smart plant managers think about the following question regarding agenda:

  What issues are top priorities for each side, how much emphasis should be put on each of these, and when should they be discussed?

- *Goals*

Goals are the desired objectives of each side. Smart plant managers think about the following question regarding goals:

What are the goals for each side, what are acceptable outcomes, and what are unacceptable outcomes?

- *Options*

  Options are solutions to a failed negotiation. Smart plant managers think about the following question regarding alternatives:

  What direction will be taken if an agreement is not reached and how can good working relationships be maintained?

Failing to listen or observe

Please consider the following for these two mistakes:

- *Listening*

  As noted earlier, some plant managers would rather hear themselves talk than listen to what the other side has to say. This can impact the outcome of negotiations...even to a point where an agreement cannot be reached. A lot more is learned by listening than talking, but some people fail to understand this fact.

- *Observing*

    Some plant managers fail to pick up on non-verbal actions from the other side. Slouched body posture, crossed arms, smiles, raised eyebrows, and head shakes are all movements that can indicate people's thoughts. This information can then be used to find common ground and reach compromises.

Failing to keep an open mind

As noted earlier, plant managers need open minds to find alternative ways of reaching agreements. However, some people are unable to think "outside of the box," and this limits their options for problem-solving.

Open-minded thinking has been a critical aspect of research, innovation, and creativity for centuries. The same philosophy needs to be applied to negotiation...but this is something that many people fail to realize.

Failing to recognize one's behavior

Some plant managers do not realize the impact of their behavior during negotiations. They need to understand that their actions are perceived by the other party in different ways...and negative perceptions can prevent an agreement from being reached.

Consider the following examples of behavior in negotiations:

- Loud people appear dominant. The other side views them as rude and aggressive.
- Quiet people appear aloof. The other side views them as having limited interest.
- Nervous people appear unprepared or inexperienced. The other side views them as having limited knowledge.
- People who do not make eye contact appear shady. The other side views them as untrustworthy.

In short, plant managers who do not recognize the impact of their behavior are damaging to themselves and their members.

Failing to hold composure

One last mistake that is often not thought about involves the aftermath of negotiations. Some people celebrate the "victory" after the negotiation is over, and this response risks alienating the other side.

Gloating is unprofessional and it makes the other side seek revenge in future negotiations. In short, plant managers need to think about the impact of their reactions to the final agreement.

Emotional intelligence

Emotional intelligence is the capacity of someone to understand the feelings of others and control their own feelings. Emotionally intelligent people hear what others are saying and react emphatically without being upset or distraught. This type of behavior is beneficial in organizations because it prevents situations from becoming emotionally charged. Based on this, it is understandable that emotionally intelligent people often rise to leadership roles in organizations.

In terms of leadership, emotional intelligence is the ability to manage feelings and understand the feelings of others. Plant managers with high emotional intelligence know what their emotions are capable of doing, and they harness their feelings to prevent negative reactions from others.

Many articles and books have been written about emotional intelligence and many more will be written in the future due to its mainstream popularity. In terms of business, the topic has generated worldwide attention due to its application in all different types of organizations. This book could expand more on emotional intelligence, but it was not written for that purpose. However, a basic understanding of the concept is necessary to see why it is so critical for plant managers.

Plant managers need to listen to, understand, and empathize with their employees. This can be very challenging, but mastering these skills often separates good plant managers from those who are not so good.

Emotional intelligence is a plant manager's ability to manage his or her own feelings and understand the feelings of others.

Plant managers with high emotional intelligence know what their emotions are capable of doing, and they harness their feelings to prevent negative reactions from others.

Emotional intelligence is a term that was developed by psychologists Peter Salovey and John Mayer...and later popularized by psychologist Daniel Goleman. Essentially, Goleman designated five major components of emotional intelligence. These components are:

Self-awareness

This refers to recognizing one's own feelings. Self-aware plant managers are able to identify and monitor their own emotions for control. They are confident and have a good sense of humor. They are also aware of how they are perceived by others.

Self-regulation

This refers to controlling reactions or impulses. Plant managers who react quickly often end up saying things that they would not have said if they thought about the situation. Self-regulation makes people conscientious about what they are saying, and it prevents them from responding in ways that elevate the negativity of conversations.

Motivation

This refers to self-motivation for self-improvement. It goes above money and status (external rewards) by focusing on things such as satisfaction and happiness (internal rewards). It also includes a strong drive to accomplish goals and objectives regardless of the circumstances. Optimism is critical for plant managers here...even when they are faced with potential failure.

Empathy

This refers to plant managers understanding other people's situations and taking a genuine interest in those situations. It often involves "walking a mile in another person's shoes" to fully comprehend their behavior and reactions. This is the most skillful component because it sometimes requires the anticipation of others' needs so the appropriate response can be made.

Social skills

This involves plant managers picking up on social cues to build relationships and work toward common goals. It requires active listening and appropriate responding to persuade others and gain their trust. It also involves team-building and collaboration as a method of working with others.

Plant managers need to realize that emotional intelligence is a great tool for preventing conflict. Not all conflict is bad because many good things come when people disagree (known as functional conflict). Without functional conflict, groupthink can result where everyone agrees because they believe it is the general consensus of the group. Groupthink prevents potential solutions from surfacing and, consequently, problems are not resolved with the best solutions. However, conflict is bad when it becomes dysfunctional. Dysfunctional conflict results in a focus on position instead of principle, and it leads to people being attacked rather than problems. Dysfunctional conflict often results in a complete breakdown of communication, and nothing constructive gets accomplished.

Emotional intelligence improves plant managers' ability to communicate constructively and collaboratively. It also helps them remain calm in challenging situations, and it prevents dysfunctional conflict from occurring. In short, emotional intelligence is needed for plant managers to perform at peak levels.

A discussion on the skill of emotional intelligence would not be complete without mentioning listening. Listening plays a big role in communication for plant managers. In fact, it might be the most important aspect of their communication because the lack of it tends to create a wealth of misunderstanding.

Listening is a process that involves plant managers focusing on what others are saying. On the surface, this might seem like an easy task...but that is typically not the case due to the barriers that are present. These barriers include noise, visual distractions, emotions, fatigue, anger, accents, language, jargon, and acronyms. All of these barriers prevent understanding and lead to misunderstanding because the message that is being sent is not comprehended.

The previous paragraph makes it seem like listening is a lost cause because it has so many barriers. Fortunately, this is not true. With a little concentration, plant managers can hear and comprehend what is being said by others. This is good because effective listening has many benefits including:

Understanding

There is no doubt that effective listening creates a better understanding of the discussion that is transpiring. Without understanding, most conversations are severely hindered. Think about holding a conversation with a friend inside a crowded bar that has loud music playing. The loud music and crowd noise create a barrier to effective listening, and the resulting lack of understanding hinders the conversation.

Efficiency

When people listen to each other, everything becomes more efficient. They understand what is being said, resulting in less confusion and fewer mistakes. In this sense, it is much easier to accomplish goals and tasks that are a part of everyday life.

Insight

When plant managers hear what is actually being said, they gather information that can be used to define a position and make decisions. This information influences behavior and brings about change that helps individuals reach the mindset where they feel the most comfortable. Plant managers who do not effectively listen fail to acquire information, and they are often left uncertain of the direction they need to take on important aspects of the conversation.

Bonding

This is likely the least known benefit of effective listening, but often it is the most important of those listed in this book. This is because trust builds when one person believes another is listening to them...and trust leads to bonding.

Conversations also become more enjoyable when effective listening is employed because there is less repeating of what has already been said. In this regard, effective listing helps people bond because speakers feel like their words are important and not easily forgotten. They do not get annoyed from being asked to repeat the words that they have just spoken, and this prevents the potential conflict that can occur when people become upset with others for an apparent lack of interest or concern.

Skilled plant managers understand that active listening means fully concentrating on the speaker while blocking out all distractions. This is a learned skill that takes work, but it can be achieved with some time and effort.

LADDER is an acronym that helps plant managers actively listen. It has been around for many years and it is often used by consultants to help people improve their listening skills. LADDER stands for the following:

L - Look at the person talking to you

Plant managers who look away from the speaker appear uninterested or bored. When this happens, speakers tend to shut down because they feel that they are not getting the proper attention paid to them. Some people even become upset because they feel insulted.

A - Ask questions

Follow-up questions need to be asked by plant managers to fully comprehend what speakers are saying. These questions should be open-ended so explanation and expansion on the subject matter are possible. For example, rather than asking an employee if she likes her job, it is better to ask her to explain what she likes and dislikes about her job. A simple yes or no does not always give enough information...just ask anyone who has been through a legal deposition.

D – Don't change the subject

Changing the subject is a very common mistake that plant managers make when they are supposed to be listening. For example, an employee is talking about the beautiful rivers she saw during a recent trip to Alaska, and the plant manager changes the subject to the beautiful Everglades he saw during a trip to Florida. The employee feels as if the spotlight has shifted from her trip to his vacation...and this is frustrating.

D – Don't interrupt

Some plant managers tend to interrupt others when they are speaking. Instead of listening, these individuals are thinking about what they are going to say next...and this interferes with their comprehension of what the speaker is saying. Interruption is sometimes necessary for clarification purposes, but it should be avoided as a general rule.

E - Emotions...control emotions

Not surprisingly, plant managers need to control their emotions when listening to others. Outbursts should be avoided because they prevent effective listening and lead to other problems such as disagreement or conflict.

R - Respond to the person speaking

Plant managers who engage themselves will listen more effectively because they are involved in the conversation. Fortunately, engagement can be accomplished without asking questions or interrupting. For example, plant managers can smile, nod their heads, raise their eyebrows, or lean forward to show interest. Additionally, simple phrases such as "I understand" or "that makes sense" can also be used as response techniques.

When listening on the telephone, the "L" may stand for limit doing other things such as typing, writing, using a calculator, trying to hold another conversation, or attempting to answer another call. Many plant managers like to perform multiple tasks, but oftentimes a telephone conversation deserves their complete attention.

Soft Skills

Soft skills and hard skills are both important for people in leadership positions. While most plant managers have mastered the hard skills necessary for their positions, many find harnessing the soft skills to be much more challenging. These two skill sets differ from each other as shown by the descriptions below.

Soft skills

Soft skills are interpersonal and they are used by people to get along with others. Examples include listening, empathy, communication, manners, etiquette, and understanding. These skills can be learned, but they are often innate and are used without a great deal of thought or practice.

Soft skills are not particular to a position, business, or industry. They can be applied to a wide variety of job types and are used by people throughout their professional careers. They are especially useful for plant managers because these individuals need to form the relationships necessary to motivate, influence, and guide others. For example, a plant manager in the automotive manufacturing business who has empathy and understanding for his employees can have similar empathy and understanding for the employees of a retail chain of health food stores if he assumes a management position in that organization.

Hard Skills

Hard skills are typically learned and can be measured and evaluated. People's proficiency with these skills is usually based on the time and effort they put into learning them. Examples include reading, writing, math, science, accounting, and economics.

Hard skills are often particular to a job, business, or industry. They are very valuable because they help people solve problems that cannot be solved by those who are unqualified. These skills are usually acquired through challenging classroom work and other types of training, but the time and effort put forth are well worth it when the skills are put into action.

One disadvantage of hard skills is the fact that they are often not applicable when leaders make career changes. For example, using the example in the soft skills description above, the strong mechanical engineering skills of the plant manager in the automotive manufacturing business will most likely not be helpful in his new management role in the retail chain of health food stores.

People with soft skills often make the most successful plant managers. Below are some important traits of soft-skilled plant managers that show why they are good at motivating others to follow them.

True listeners

Much of what humans learn is acquired through listening. Reading, writing, and speaking account for some learning, but listening is the biggest factor.

Unfortunately, people comprehend less than half of what they hear. This means the majority of time spent listening is wasted...at least from a learning standpoint. Based on this, it seems rather obvious that people would try to improve their listening skills. However, this is typically not the case, and that is why effective listeners often rise to plant management roles in organizations.

Some of the benefits of listening include those shown below.

- *Understanding*

  There is no doubt that effective listening creates a better understanding of the discussion that is transpiring. Without understanding, most conversations are severely hindered. Think about holding a conversation with a friend inside a crowded bar that has loud music playing. The loud music and crowd noise create a barrier to effective listening, and the resulting lack of understanding hinders the conversation.

- *Efficiency*

When people listen to each other, everything becomes more efficient. They understand what is being said, and that understanding results in less confusion and mistakes. In this sense, it is much easier to accomplish goals and tasks that are a part of everyday life.

- *Insight*

When people hear what is actually being said, they gather information that can be used to define their position and make decisions. This information influences behavior and brings about change that helps individuals reach the mindset where they feel the most comfortable. People who do not effectively listen fail to acquire information, and they are often left uncertain of the direction they need to take on important aspects of the conversation. In short, people who listen effectively gain insight that benefits them.

- *Bonding*

This is likely the least known benefit of effective listening, but it is often the most important because trust builds when one person believes another is listening to them...and trust leads to bonding.

Conversations also become more enjoyable when effective listening is employed because there is less repeating of what has already been said. In this regard, effective listing helps people bond because speakers feel like their words are important and not easily forgotten. They do not get annoyed from being asked to repeat the words that they have just spoken, and this prevents the potential conflict that can occur when people become upset with others for an apparent lack of interest or concern.

Soft-skilled plant managers do an excellent job of listening. They stand out among good listeners because they are truly focused on what others are saying with the hope of learning something new. In other words, they are more than just empathetic and understanding...they are also interested.

Soft-skilled plant managers also know that there is a difference between hearing what someone says and actually listening to what they say. They know how to listen and use that ability to get people to truly feel as if they are being heard.

Conflict resolvers

It can be said with confidence plant managers are going to experience conflict among the people they oversee.

A harmonious and disagreement-free workplace would be nice, but it is not reality regardless of the type or size of the organization being led.

Contrary to what some people believe, conflict is not all bad. In fact, some conflict is good because change evolves from it. Without disagreement, the status quo would remain the same and nothing would improve. However, conflict can get out of control and become dysfunctional. Dysfunctional conflict is destructive because position becomes more important than principle, and people are attacked instead of problems. These personal attacks are always negative, and nothing constructive gets accomplished.

When dysfunctional conflict occurs, it needs to be resolved. Soft-skilled plant managers realize the importance of focusing on the problem rather than the people in the conflict, and they work toward a resolution using mitigation strategies that soften the harsh effects and save face for all parties involved.

Mind openers

Mind-opening plant managers are individuals who are able to open up the minds of their employees so they will accept things that are outside of their comfort zones. This is a skill that most people do not have and it is very valuable for getting employees to embrace change.

Change is difficult for most people to embrace because it requires them to think or behave differently than they have in the past. They have to leave familiar territory and enter into something unfamiliar while not really knowing what lies ahead. For example, Maria changes careers and enters a manufacturing plant where she must leave behind what she knows and take on new roles and responsibilities. She realizes that her work world is going to change, but she does not know how drastic that change will be. Questions flow through her mind causing her to worry about the future. Examples of these questions include the following:

- Will she understand her new job so she can perform as expected?
- Will she have the respect of coworkers who know that she has no direct experience?
- Will she be able to adjust to a different work environment?
- Will she be able to transfer her skills to her new career?

All of the above questions stem from a fear of the unknown. Overcoming that fear is a daunting task for Maria, but a soft skilled plant manager can make the process much more fluid and comfortable for her by listening to her, showing empathy for her concerns, and offering support for getting her through the initial phases. Once she settles into the position and has a better understanding of her work environment and job responsibilities, her fears will ease and she will become a productive member of the organization.

Mind opening is one of the most important traits of soft-skilled plant managers due to the resistance that so many people have to change. They will go to great lengths to avoid leaving the areas of comfort that they have established over time, and they require help outside of themselves to move in a different direction...even if that direction leads to making their jobs easier in the future.

Acceptors

Good plant managers act as mind openers for others, but they also need to be open-minded themselves. This means they have to accept the reality of their surroundings. In fact, it is difficult for people to become effective leaders in organizations if they do not accept the reality of situations around them. Adolph Hitler, for example, forced his military personnel to fight till the death even though they had limited equipment and supplies and World War II was at a point where Germany had no chance of emerging victorious. He refused to see his country's defeat as it unfolded around him, regardless of what he personally witnessed or was told by his top aides. In the end, he failed miserably in his leadership role and millions of people were killed or had their lives negatively disrupted.

Hitler, however, was not known as a soft-skilled leader. Empathy and understanding are two traits that do not come to mind when thinking about him and, as shown in the preceding paragraph, he was not a particularly good

182

listener. However, many plant managers do have soft skills, and those skills allow them to accept the reality that occurs around them. They hear what other people are telling them, show respect for their opinions and comments, and act accordingly based on an analysis of the entire situation. They experience success in leadership roles because they have the ability to:

- *Accept problems*

  Like other leaders, soft-skilled plant managers understand that problems are going to arise that need to be resolved. However, their skill sets set them apart from other plant managers because they have the ability to take things in stride and move toward a resolution without exaggerating the impact of the problem or placing blame on others. On the surface, this ability might not appear to be of any great importance. However, appearances can be deceiving as is the case here because problem exaggeration and blame games in organizations result in compounded issues including unnecessary stress, mental fatigue, fear of job loss, and, if allowed to fester, an exodus of good employees.

  The acceptance of problems also helps speed up the time required to find a solution because less time is spent arguing over who is at fault. In business, time is money...and money is what typically drives the bottom line.

- *Accept criticism*

The acceptance of criticism does not come easy for many people. In fact, some individuals are simply not able to handle any type of critique of their actions even though the critique might be constructive. These people cannot get past the feeling of being personally attacked so they refuse to accept suggestions for improvement and, consequently, fail to get better.

Soft-skilled plant managers allow themselves to be criticized by others without becoming emotionally charged or seeking vengeance against their accusers. They avoid reacting in a hostile or aggressive manner to criticism, and they do not assume that those doing the criticizing are automatically wrong.

The acceptance of criticism helps plant managers in two different ways. First, it allows them to improve their leadership skills by understanding their shortcomings and using that understanding to strengthen their weak areas. Second, it improves their image in the minds of others because they are not viewed as being know-it-alls who can do no wrong.

- *Accept opinion*

Everyone has an opinion and rarely, if ever, are those opinions the exact same for a topic of discussion. Keeping this in mind, people should understand that others are not always going to agree with their thinking so they should show respect for differing opinions. Unfortunately, this is not always the case...especially when the discussion includes race, religion, or politics. However, regardless of the discussion topic, some people always believe their opinion is right and they refuse to spend any time entertaining the possibility that others might be correct.

Soft-skilled plant managers respect the opinions of others. They do this by understanding that opinions are nothing more than personal thoughts. They also move away from trying to rationalize others' opinions in their own minds because they know that this might not be possible to do.

The acceptance of others' opinions is important for plant managers because they open themselves up to new concepts and ideas that they might not think of on their own. It also prevents them from being surrounded by people who never want to disagree or express their own thoughts and ideas.

Soft-skilled plant managers keep their minds open at all times. They pay attention to their surroundings and know that others possess a world of information that is of no value to them if they choose to ignore it. Quite simply, they view their minds as parachutes because those minds "do not work unless they are open."

Change implementers

Change is inevitable for organizations or they will become stagnant and, over time, cease to exist. Change is important for organizational prosperity, and astute plant managers understand this importance better than anyone else. They can visualize what needs to be done for the growth of their organizations. That visualization, however, requires implementation before the change becomes a reality...and only the best plant managers successfully complete that implementation.

Change implementation requires mind-opening skills to get people to buy into the idea of doing something differently, but it also requires the ability to move the process forward and help it take root until it becomes a normal part of the status quo. Soft-skilled plant managers have this ability due to their influential personalities and communicative styles. They are able to take employees down new trails that lead to unfamiliar territories because they understand people. Their empathetic nature provides support for those who are unsure of their own actions or the actions of others as the change takes place. The comfort level experienced by employees allows them to become an active part of the implementation process which greatly aids plant managers in reaching organizational goals and objectives.

In a nutshell, soft-skilled plant managers are able to identify where and when change is needed, but, even more importantly, they can implement that change so it becomes part of their employees' everyday routines. The key to this implementation is effective communication, something that comes naturally to plant managers with soft skills.

Motivators

The phrase "location, location, location" is frequently used to describe real estate transactions because the value of a property is largely based on the area where that property is located. The same idea relates to plant managers when trying to get people to follow them, but the phrase is different. Leadership is based on "motivation, motivation, motivation" because people need to be motivated to do what those at the top want them to do.

Employees need motivation for a variety of different reasons. One person needs it for undergoing change while another needs it for confidence-building and a third needs it to feel appreciated. However, regardless of the reason, workers require motivation at work and good plant managers provide that motivation so those workers can see the value of themselves and their accomplishments.

Soft skilled plant managers are in tune with the needs of their employees and they know how to motivate those employees to work toward achieving organizational goals and objectives. They use praise as a tool for getting people to buy into basic management philosophies, they offer support by asking employees what they need to properly perform their jobs, and they provide feedback so employees know where they need to improve.

Without a doubt, soft-skilled plant managers are the best leaders for motivating employees. Their personalities are naturally geared toward treating people with respect and showing compassion for them as they work through the everyday challenges of their jobs. In short, they know how to inspire people because they understand their personal and professional needs.

Trust builders

As many people are aware, trust-building is a challenging endeavor. It takes time and effort to create the relationships necessary to establish trust, and that trust can be broken with a single action.

Communication is the biggest factor involved in building trust, and it starts with leadership. Employees lose trust when plant managers do not communicate with them. They want truthful information about their organizations so they know what is happening within them. Without leadership communication, employees are lost without a guide.

Trust also leads to the establishment of culture. Every organization has unique experiences, philosophies, behaviors, norms, and values. They also have specific methods and patterns for interacting with suppliers, customers, employees, and the community. When combined, these attributes define an organization and make up its culture.

Culture starts at the top of an organization and works its way down to lower-level employees. Employees help establish behaviors and norms, but they do not have the same power as those in the upper levels of the established hierarchy. Top ranking members are the only people who have the authority, influence, and control needed to create the overall culture of the organization.

Plant managers need employees to trust them or they will not achieve the goals that they have set for their organizations. In fact, trust is one of the most important aspects of leadership because it is difficult, if not impossible, to repair once it is broken.

Employees trust plant managers with soft skills because these leaders are empathetic and think before they react. They think about how they would feel if something was done to them that they are about to do to others. For example, before telling employees they are doing a bad job, they think of things that they are also doing well to mitigate the harshness of the reprimands.

Soft-skilled plant managers also understand the importance of maintaining trust once it has been established. They know that employees who lose faith in their actions will also lose faith in their organizations.

If this happens, then those organizations risk failure and might cease to exist.

Soft-skilled plant managers have an advantage over other plant managers when it comes to trust. They behave in ways that draw their employees toward them and help those employees believe in the goals and objectives that they have established. Hard skills are great for many aspects of management in organizations, but they cannot compare to the positive effects of soft skills.

Team players

Teams are the major building blocks of many different types of organizations. They have replaced individuals in an attempt to satisfy complex customer demands and resolve internal issues. They utilize personnel who help solve problems faster and more accurately. These personnel are selected based on their position, skill, knowledge, and capacity to lead others. The assembled team is well equipped to find solutions to problems based on their experience, understanding, and capability.

The advantages of teams make it important for plant managers to work in, with, and around them. Some of the major advantages are discussed below.

- *Synergy*

This might be the biggest advantage of teams because every member can exchange thoughts and entertain others' perspectives. Each employee has unique strengths that add diversity to the team, and the differing viewpoints contribute to the overall effectiveness. The synergy involved improves decision-making and helps the team reach goals within limited time frames. Soft skilled plant managers add to this synergy by motivating team members to express their thoughts and ideas.

- *Efficiency*

Teams are able to move faster and more effectively than individuals acting alone. This is because they make the most of members' individual strengths and talents. In areas where some people are weak, others are strong...and their combined efforts work together to solve problems.

The best part about the efficiency of a team is that it gets better as the team bonds. Over time, members learn the strengths of others in the group and utilize those strengths where and when they are needed. Soft skilled plant managers use their communication skills to improve bonding between members; thereby increasing the efficiency of the team as a whole.

- *Flexibility*

Different personalities on a team help the team accept change. Some people find change challenging or stressful while others embrace it. This is because people react differently to the same situations based on their perceptions, and those perceptions give teams the flexibility needed to accept change. Since soft-skilled plant managers do well with change and change implementation, they are a big plus for the flexibility of teams.

- *Idea generation*

People have different experiences that add to the way they think about things. Team members' individual thoughts generate unique ideas that can be bounced off the rest of the group for problem-solving. This process generates the best ideas because they are evaluated by everyone before being implemented as solutions. In terms of idea generation, soft-skilled plant managers help team members realize the importance of their contributions based on their unique experiences.

- *Divided responsibilities*

Teams divide responsibilities between group members, and this prevents individual employees from being overloaded with work. It also allows members to support each other through cooperation and mutual understanding. In short, dividing responsibilities alleviates the stress associated with being completely responsible for a project. Soft-skilled plant managers understand the importance of keeping stress levels manageable and they take action to assure those levels do not become excessive.

The above advantages show why "team players" are important in organizations. When teams succeed, all members are rewarded rather than individuals, and the end result is increased motivation and job satisfaction for everyone.

Unfortunately, team players can be difficult to find in organizations because employees typically have much more interest in helping themselves than they do in helping others. This might seem rather harsh, but it is true...especially when companies are cutting costs by hiring fewer people and putting pressure on existing employees to do more.

Soft skilled plant managers do well managing teams, but they also are excellent team players. They enjoy giving credit to others and know when it is more important to listen rather than act. They allow informal rules to develop within the teams without interjection. These rules guide members on how to share resources and responsibilities, and they provide a roadmap for accomplishing goals and objectives.

One negative aspect of teams is the fact that individuals sometimes lose their creativity. Soft-skilled plant managers understand the need for creativity and work with members to allow for it. They often sacrifice their own thoughts and ideas to entertain the thoughts and ideas of others so everyone can contribute and feel part of the decision-making process.

Soft-skilled plant managers also realize that team members require a time period to adjust to each other's work styles and personalities. This period is known as a learning curve, and it is a problem because team members are not productive during it. Valuable resources are tied up during this process, and that can be costly. However, astute plant managers allow it to naturally take place since the end result is worth the time and money spent.

Political

The best and sometimes most important skill in this book is saved for last. Plant managers need to have political skills based on the fact that they have to deal with so many different people at so many different levels of authority. They need to navigate through different personalities, cultures, religions, and beliefs while not offending these individuals and accomplishing organizational goals and objectives. This is no small task...especially for plant managers who do not have a good grasp of political correctness.

Political correctness is a term that is familiar to most people. They understand its importance, but it also makes them feel uneasy because it presents the dichotomy of "damned if you do, damned if you don't." More specifically, people who choose to be politically correct risk losing the true meaning of their statements while those who choose to ignore political correctness risk offending others. This concern for political correctness has been around for a long time, but it is a major worry for plant managers because they want to avoid miscommunication and lawsuits.

Plant managers need to be aware that political correctness exists. They must understand that it affects organizational culture in positive and negative ways as follows:

Positives

- *Good model for young people* – Young employees are influenced by coworkers who are older and more experienced. If older workers show respect for the people they work with, then the younger workers will likely follow the same path. Plant managers must be proactive and encourage older employees to have a positive influence on their younger coworkers. The need to realize that those younger workers represent the future of the organization.

- *Promotes tolerance* – Mutual respect and understanding are necessary for people to work together and accept others. Plant managers need to understand the importance of tolerance for accomplishing goals and objectives.

- *Eliminates prejudice* – Bias is rarely, if ever, good in organizations. When employees judge each other negatively, the entire plant is impacted. Plant managers must understand that prejudice today could lead to stereotyping that becomes the norm in the future.

Negatives

- *Restricts the truth* - Employees are afraid to speak their minds for fear of being labeled insensitive, uncaring, archaic, ignorant, bigoted, or racist. Plant managers have to realize the truth is necessary to sort facts from fiction and solve problems.

- *Creates hypersensitivity* – Negative emotions can surface that lead to irrational decision-making, warring factions, dysfunctional conflict, or organizational "witch hunts." Plant managers need to know that these types of problems affect the efficiency of the manufacturing plant.

- *Lawsuits* - Political correctness can lead to legal action being taken against individuals or organizations. Plant managers need to understand that lawsuits cost money....regardless of whether they are won or lost.

An entire book could be written on the reasons why political correctness exists, but it effectively boils down to employees communicating without offending each other. Employees are capable of offending each other while discussing a variety of different topics. However, discussions involving race, religion, politics, sexual orientation, and gender (also known as sensitive discussion) are the most likely to evoke emotional responses and turn people against each other. Offense taken from these particular topics can lead to many problems including terminations and lawsuits. Plant managers need to understand that political correctness allows employees to take part in sensitive discussions without offending each other...and the benefits will showcase themselves.

Plant managers also need to be aware that sensitive discussions evolve over time. Something that was politically correct at one time might be considered taboo today. For example, when the welfare system was developed it was positively thought of as temporary assistance for people until they were able to find gainful employment. People were thought of as using the system for help, and they were not offended when others categorized them as welfare recipients. Today, some people on welfare are viewed as using the system so they do not have work. These individuals are thought of as abusing government assistance, and they are offended when they are categorized by others as welfare recipients...and it is not politically correct to label them as such.

When the wrong choice of words is used during a workplace discussion, it can offend people and trigger angry or emotional responses. Obviously, this is not always the case, but some employees do get offended and that offense can be prevented by using politically correct terminology.

One last aspect of political correctness that warrants discussion involves organizational culture. Every manufacturing facility has unique experiences, philosophies, behaviors, norms, and values. They also have specific methods and patterns for interacting with suppliers, customers, employees, and the community. When combined, these attributes define an organization and make up its culture.

Plant managers must understand the power of culture...and the fact that they are one of the biggest influences on it. Conforming to the culture is important for raises, promotions, and other accolades. Those who choose to be non-conformists often end up on the outside. Some non-conformists leave the organization on their own terms because they cannot deal with the culture, while others are terminated because they cannot adjust. Either way, they experience the power of organizational culture and understand that it is difficult to change.

Organizational culture provides guidelines for productivity, performance, quality, and political correctness. Manufacturing facilities have documented policies and procedures in place to

This is likely the most well-known area of HRM because most people associate human resource departments with the hiring process. Human resource personnel select candidates, interview them, and make decisions about whether or not they are a good fit for the organization.

Plant managers must be involved with the recruitment process because they know what they need in terms of skills and experience. Their knowledge helps establish job specifications which is especially important for newly developed positions because there is no information available.

Plant managers can also contribute to the strategies used to promote job openings. Who is the job geared toward? Will the job be open to internal candidates only or can anyone apply? Will outside agencies be utilized to promote the opening? Answers to these questions provide a method by which potential candidates can be viewed for interviews.

Last, but certainly not least, plant managers can help reduce the pool of candidates by asking questions designed to uncover information that might not show on a resume. Leadership and interpersonal abilities are brought to light, and specific personality testing can also be used. Some plant managers, especially those with a psychology background, take the personality aspect of job fit very seriously because people's traits have been found to predict their behavior at work. Testing is utilized to determine how individuals work alone, work in teams, and work in specific environments. In other words, it shows how potential employees will fit into the culture of the organization. While personality testing is not completely reliable, it does provide insight into the selection process that cannot be obtained by reading resumes or interviewing candidates.

Compensation

This refers to the compensation employees receive for the work they perform. It can come in many different forms including pay, bonuses, commission, retirement plans, profit-sharing, stock ownership, and benefits. Employees want job satisfaction, and money always seems to play a role in finding that satisfaction. As most plant managers are aware, money is often one of the most important aspects of employment, and it is a major reason why workers remain at their current employer or leave for other positions.

Specific types of pay and compensation are listed below.

Salary

This type of pay involves a set amount of money for a certain period of time. Typically, the money is based on one year of work. This wage does not normally change until management decides a change is justified. Usually, employees' salaries go up based on their increased value to the organization. However, salaries can also go down if management believes employees are not producing enough to warrant their wages.

Hourly

Employees who are compensated hourly receive an agreed-upon amount of money per hour of work. There is no guaranteed amount of money that these employees make in a year because the number of hours worked depends on organizational needs or customer demand. However, unions have changed the rules for many workplaces by guaranteeing minimum hours per week for hourly employees.

Typically increases in money per hour for hourly employees are based on time intervals or the ability to perform certain job functions. Again, unions have intervened and implemented rules that need to be followed in some workplaces. These rules guarantee employees' wage increases after a certain amount of time with the organization. Rarely do hourly wages go down, but this can happen if concessions are implemented.

Commission

Commission pay is typically used for salespeople. Often times it involves a base salary plus a commission that is based on the total sales achieved. In short, increased sales result in increased commission.

Commission does not necessarily have to be monetary. Depending on the leadership of the organization, it can also be used for purchasing:

- A company vehicle
- An upgrade of a benefit package
- Additional time off or vacation
- A contribution to a retirement plan

- Company stock

Bonus

Bonus pay is money given to people at the end of a specific amount of time. It is typically based on performance, and there are a variety of ways to calculate the amount of money paid out. The bonus can be a percentage of employees' pay, an amount based on the profitability of the organization, a number based on employees' goal achievements, or an arbitrary figure determined by management. Regardless of the method used for determination of the dollar value, the objective of a bonus is to reward employees with additional income.

Piece-rate

This compensation pays employees a pre-determined amount of money for a specific amount of work. People earn income based on their total output regardless of the amount of time they spend doing the job.

Merit

This is a traditional type of compensation. Essentially, employee performance is evaluated using an appraisal system, and compensation is adjusted based on the results.

Skill

This compensation is based on employee expertise rather than on more traditional factors such as seniority or specific achievements. Essentially, skill pay is based on worker performance in relation to core competencies such as multi-tasking and leadership.

Profit-sharing

This type of compensation is provided in addition to salary, hourly wages, bonuses, and commissions. It is based on the profitability of the organization, and management determines the amount of the contribution. The money is often paid out when employees leave the organization or retire.

Gain sharing

Gain sharing is similar to profit-sharing with some distinct differences. Both programs are designed for employees to share in the success of organizations. However, contributions to gain-sharing programs are not based on profitability. Instead, employees need to meet designated goals to receive payouts. Typically these goals involve productivity increases from one period to the next.

Employee stock ownership

This type of compensation is part of a benefit program where employees can purchase stock. The price of the stock is typically below the market value, and this makes it easier to purchase for workers.

Benefits

Employee benefits are compensation in addition to an agreed-upon wage. They encompass a variety of different components and are based on many factors. However, the major benefits referred to in this section are health insurance, dental insurance, life insurance, vacation, paid days off, and retirement programs.

Work-life balance

Work-life balance involves accomplishing work-related goals while enjoying life outside of work. As people's lives become busier and more hectic, they begin to realize the importance of work-life balance. Time is limited, and different things need to take priority at different times in life. People need to work to sustain a certain lifestyle, but they also need the time to enjoy that lifestyle.

Astute plant managers involve themselves in employees' compensation because it is useful for keeping employees happy and motivated while reducing turnover. It also impacts the financial bottom line...something that factors into most plant managers' performance evaluations.

Training

Astute plant managers understand that training is a process where information is provided for educational purposes. Employees acquire knowledge and skills that can be used for enhancing their job performance. They get better at their jobs, thereby becoming more efficient and effective. Additionally, training leads to employees requiring less direct supervision. They are able to do their work with minimal guidance due to the autonomy that training instills. This means supervisors can focus on other aspects of their jobs without the threat of employee mistakes being made due to misunderstanding or lack of knowledge.

Production employees need training to understand how to do their jobs properly. Plant managers need to understand that part of that training involves safety because, without safety, employees risk injury. They enter unknown territory and are unsure how to prevent potentially dangerous situations...and how to get out of those situations if they become a reality.

Training starts with showing workers how to properly operate equipment. This involves understanding body positioning, ergonomics, fatigue, distractions, safety features, and shutoffs in the event of an emergency. This might seem rather basic or simple to some readers of this book, but many times it is the exact opposite. In crises, employees have only seconds to react, and often they do not react properly in terms of limiting injury to themselves or others.

Plant managers need to realize that proper safety training cannot be conducted if the trainers do not possess the required skills to teach others. Obviously, those skills involve understanding plant operations and the machinery being used. Trainers need to be able to teach employees how to behave to prevent unsafe situations and how to act in the event of an emergency. However, one often overlooked skill of instructors is their ability to assess the people being trained. The need to understand the skills and capabilities of the plant employees and alter the course design based on a well-thought analysis. For example, skilled tradesmen have typically already had safety training, so they will have a good comprehension of the material being presented. Conversely, that level of comprehension is not always the same for new employees or those who have never had any formal training. These individuals might need extra time and explanation to absorb the information...and the trainer needs to realize and react to this need.

Common barriers to the proper training of manufacturing employees include the following;

Language

This is one of the biggest barriers so it deserves to be mentioned first. Many production facilities employ workers whose first language is not English. This results in misunderstanding and a lack of comprehension when safety training is conducted only in English. By no means does this mean these employees are "dumb" or incapable of learning. They may be very smart and eager to learn...but that learning is only accomplished in their native tongues.

Smart plant managers understand that they can hire translators if the money is available to do so. However, if money is a concern, then coworkers who speak the same language can be utilized to translate. Additionally, written documents can be translated for free on various internet websites. These translations are typically not perfect, but the information that they do provide is better than nothing at all.

Lack of information

Regardless of the comprehension or understanding of the trainees, they will not learn what they need to know if information is left out. Some trainers assume the trainees already have an understanding of a particular concept, so they skip over it and move into the next part of the course. This might not be common, but it does occur and that is why it is listed as a barrier to training. There is an old saying that states "never assume anything." This saying has great application in safety training because improper assumptions can lead to injury or death.

Plant managers need to assume employees know very little in terms of safety. Trainers should start with the easiest aspects of training and work up to the more complex topics. Although this might be boring for some of the participants, it could prevent injury and/or save lives.

Lack of clarity

Many employees are afraid of looking "dumb" or "stupid" in front of their coworkers, so they avoid asking questions for a better understanding of what they are attempting to learn. This presents a situation that does not resolve itself...and trainees leave without having a full understanding of what they have been taught.

Astute plant managers realize that smaller training groups often help employees feel more comfortable asking questions that they believe might embarrass them in front of their co-workers. Another solution is to allow employees an opportunity to post anonymous questions during the training that are only seen by the trainer. Privacy is a concern of some trainees, and that concern needs to be taken into consideration to assure proper learning.

Lack of follow-up

This barrier is unique because it takes place after the training is completed. Once safety procedures have been put in place, they need to be followed up on to make sure they are successful. Management often overlooks follow-up by failing to post reminders in the plant or neglecting to see if the training is working.

Plant managers should have signs posted around machinery to point out specific safety procedures, posters can be hung on walls throughout the plant to promote general safety, and periodic emails or memos can be sent to employees to remind them about the importance of safety. Additionally, supervisors need to walk around and make mental notes of what is happening in terms of safety. Are employees following established protocols? If not, then they might need to be retrained verbally or in a more formal setting.

Evaluation

Employees are typically evaluated by people in higher positions. Sometimes that evaluation is informal, such as an evaluation by an owner of a small company. Other times it is a documented formality that occurs regularly. Either way, evaluations are a method of determining the worth of employees to their organizations. Promotions, demotions, and terminations are often based on them, and wages are adjusted accordingly.

Human resource personnel are usually an active part of the evaluation process. They make sure a structured format is followed to address important aspects of the employee's performance. This format ensures that an employee is meeting expectations in a timely and effective manner. If expectations are being met, then the review can be rather brief. However, if expectations are not being met, then the review can last substantially longer and include an improvement plan that details specific requirements and time frames for completion.

Plant managers should monitor the process of improvement plans to assure employees are doing what is expected of them. This process might appear to be derogatory because people's shortcomings come to the surface and are dwelled upon...but that is simply not always the case. In fact, improvement plans can be very constructive, and their benefits include the following:

- They help employees achieve goals that they were unable to accomplish alone.
- They document success that builds employee confidence.
- They help employees realize that they have more to contribute to the organization.
- They allow employees to maintain their jobs while paving the way for future compensation increases.

In short, employee evaluations are important because help organizations accomplish goals and objectives. Human resource people are responsible for much of this process, but plant managers should keep an eye on the improvement processes to assure they are working as designed.

Legalities

This is where high levels of expertise are required because mistakes can be very costly to organizations. Human resource people uphold policies and procedures, including disciplinary action and terminations, and must understand the legal aspects of situations or they risk the possibility of lawsuits. For example, human resource personnel might terminate an employee for stealing based on witness accounts of the situation. However, if there is no video of the actual theft, then it might be hard to prove in court if the employee files a lawsuit. If the company loses the lawsuit, they might have to hire the employee back with retroactive pay in addition to paying attorney fees on both sides. If the company wins the lawsuit, they still have to pay its own attorney fees. In short, plant managers should understand the legalities involved to prevent firing employees without the necessary proof or documentation.

The above reasons show why plant managers should involve themselves with HRM. Let's expand upon this discussion by examining the specific goals of plant managers in terms of human resource departments. These goals are as follows:

Compliance

Plant managers need to understand that one of the major objectives of HRM is to help organizations avoid legal problems and the fines associated with them. They diligently work to keep companies in compliance with all applicable rules and regulations. This entails making sure government rules and regulations are followed. For example, there are many OSHA (Occupational Safety and Health Administration) requirements that companies must adhere to or risk the consequences. The United States Department of Labor established OSHA in 1970 with the sole purpose of enforcing laws in industrial and commercial businesses. These laws were created in response to workplace injuries and fatalities that occurred in the US. Companies that do not adhere to the rules can be fined...and those fines can exceed six figures if the findings are severe enough. HRM safety specialists promote safety awareness in workplaces when employees are working around dangerous machines or hazardous chemicals. Their goal is to keep organizations in compliance with OSHA guidelines so workers are safe and lawsuits and fines are avoided.

Along the same lines, human resource departments work to comply with all labor and wage laws. There are state and federal laws that apply to minimum wage, overtime, child labor, right to work, family medical leave, and other work-related issues. Plant managers need to have a general understanding of these laws to help human resource departments keep their organizations in compliance.

HRM also has a goal of preventing discrimination and harassment. They strive to uphold equal opportunity requirements, promote diversity, and prevent problems from occurring. Accomplishing this goal saves money, but it also has an effect on the perception of organizations. Plant managers need to be well aware that the public does not like it when they read about organizations that allow discrimination or harassment. This activity is illegal, and it results in the company being perceived as unethical.

One last HRM objectively applies to unionized facilities. Grievances related to seniority, overtime, wages, job responsibilities, and other aspects of work need to be addressed...and human resource people have a goal of resolving them as quickly and efficiently as possible. They want rules in the contract followed, and plant managers can help make sure this happens.

Commitment

This is one of the most difficult goals of human resource personnel because it is based on individual perception...and every individual is different. HRM wants all employees to be committed to their jobs and their employer. This helps organizations run more efficiently, and it relieves some of the stress experienced by human resource people.

To encourage commitment, astute plant managers get involved with employees and their supervisors. They work with employees so their voices are heard. Workers who have attention paid to them are more committed to their jobs because they feel like they are an active part of the company. This is supported by the now-famous Hawthorne Studies conducted by Elton Mayo and Fritz Roethlisberger in the 1920s. These studies show that, regardless of the work environment, employees are more productive and engaged when management pays attention to them and involves them in decision-making processes. Human resource personnel also work with supervisors to improve their communication skills and help them become more empathetic toward employees. Emotional intelligence research started by Daniel Goleman has shown that supervisor empathy is critical for getting employees to become more productive and committed.

In short, the goal of plant managers is not just to help human resources departments hire people who are qualified and have the right fit. It is also to get employees involved and make them feel a productive part of the workplace so they become committed to their jobs and their employer. Committed employees tend to remain with their organizations for long periods of time...and longevity fuels the prosperity of organizations.

Diversity and Ethics

Many organizations, especially those that are global, are made up of employees with a wide variety of backgrounds, skills, and experiences. Moat plant managers know that this diversity is good for improving their organizations as a whole, but it can lead to legal and ethical concerns. People with different cultural values, customs, religious beliefs, and social norms can offend each other without even knowing it...especially if the organization is global. Bribery, for example, might be considered unethical in the United States, but it is an accepted practice in some other nations. Along the same lines, derogatory treatment of women in business might be acceptable in certain areas of the globe, but it is illegal in the United States.

Plant managers need to assist HRM to make their organizations diverse while upholding ethical and legal standards. They must make sure that employee differences are understood and respected. This is done using awareness programs that include emails, newsletters, manuals, or programs that address culture, spirituality, customs, and social norms of the different groups of people that need to work together to accomplish organizational objectives. Achievement of this goal is critical because it prevents conflict and workplace violence that can potentially be fatal.

Improvement

Plant managers and human resource personnel have a goal of continuous improvement. They want to get better so their companies run more effectively and efficiently. However, unlike other departments in organizations, the improvements made by human resource personnel are geared toward bettering every area of the business. For example, the quality control department of a food manufacturer puts an entire day's production of potato chips on hold because they do not meet quality standards. As a consequence, the production department needs to work overtime to remake the product. The action taken by quality control personnel looks good for their department, but it hurts the production aspect of the business. At the same time, the human resource department of the food manufacturer announces a training program geared to improve the active listening skills of supervisors. This program helps all supervisors understand the needs of their employees so the organization can operate more efficiently; thereby reducing some of the headaches of plant managers.

Human resource personnel attempt to improve all areas of companies including recruitment, training, legalities, ethics, compensation, safety, and healthcare. These areas need to progressively get better for the organization to grow and prosper...and plant managers need to provide support for HRM efforts.

Organizational development

Organizational development (also known as OD) is a rather broad and sometimes misunderstood subject. It involves organizational behavior, technology, management, training, and movement into new markets. It improves virtually all aspects of business operations by overhauling the way organizations operate at all levels. In short, OD is an action-oriented process that helps organizations accomplish goals by getting employees to accept and embrace the changes necessary to do so.

Organizational development should not be confused with human resource development. Both concepts help organizations achieve goals, but human resource development promotes the growth of employees while organizational development promotes the growth of systems and processes. In short, human resource development has a micro focus while organizational development focuses on broader issues. This macro emphasis makes organizational development unique because it works to change the behavior of everything in organizations, as opposed to more traditional planning that is put in place to change specific aspects of workplaces.

Plant managers need to understand organizational development because it is important for any workplace undergoing change. It facilitates the change process while focusing on improvement at all levels of organizations. It finds the best fit for all employees regardless of their education, experience, position, or authority

The concept of organizational development stemmed from human relations studies conducted in the early 1900s. Researchers were looking at interpersonal relationships in organizations and realized that processes and structures impacted the ways employees behaved. Their behavior was shaped by different forms of motivation that they derived from the environment. Their actions were noticeably influenced by their workplaces, especially when those workplaces were undergoing change. This led to the more recent work in OD that aligns people with the changes that their organizations are going through or need to undergo. Organizational development is more important to plant managers today than it ever was in the past due to the rapid expansion of technology and the fact that global competition is now becoming the norm.

Smart plant managers know that organizational development is constantly re-inventing itself due to the challenges involved with managing change in modern companies. For example, employee feelings and emotions are now a part of the process, but they were never considered in the past. As discussed earlier, emotional intelligence is important and factors into the way plant managers implement and manage change. Information technology (also known as IT) is another factor that needs to be incorporated into OD. The wealth of material provided by new and emerging IT is overwhelming to some workers, causing them to experience the negative effects of information overload.

So, how does the process of organizational development work in manufacturing? It starts by analyzing the needs of organizations and then incorporating those needs into an action plan for change. This plan has a goal of organization-wide improvement, and it includes the following stages:

Set goals

Every plan starts with goals. Organizational development goals typically consist of improved efficiency, higher productivity, better quality, and increased profits. Essentially, these goals are somewhat diversified to improve all areas of the organization. These goals are important because they guide OD throughout the entire process.

Involve employees

Employee involvement is critical for organizational development, and it is what separates OD from other improvement programs. Workers get involved in a wide variety of activities, and their input is just as important as the input received from management. Employees are involved in the entire process, and their decisions and actions lead to continuous improvement.

Restructure

This is where the actual changes take place. Organizations cannot continue to operate the way they have been operating, so they restructure their processes and procedures. This usually involves the realignment of management and reassignment of employees. The objective is to find a better fit for everyone in the organization to achieve maximum efficiency.

Train

Once the changes have been made, employees need to be educated on best practices for their new job assignments. This requires training for all employees. Training has multiple benefits because it helps workers perform at optimal levels, makes their jobs easier, and prevents them from developing the negative attitudes that stem from misunderstanding or fear of the unknown.

Assess

After employees have been trained, the organization should start to see improvement. Now, plant management needs to assess the results of the organizational development by measuring the improvement. Profitability and productivity are often measured quantitatively with numbers, but improved morale and job satisfaction need to be measured qualitatively using surveys or other methods that tap the employees' workplace perceptions. If improvement is shown, then the OD program is working. However, if the improvement is very little or none, then more changes need to be made.

Organizational development plans revolve around groups rather than individuals. The thinking here is that groups impact organizational culture much more than individuals. This means plant managers need to make sure that groups are well-organized, goal-oriented, and driven to complete tasks. All members need to understand their roles and follow through on their responsibilities.

Since organizational development is about change, it is needed for many different change-related reasons related to plant management. Mergers and acquisitions, product modifications, price adjustments, management realignment, downsizing, rightsizing, training, and image revisions are all areas where OD is needed. The following examines three of these areas (downsizing, image revisions, and mergers and acquisitions) while showing how OD is put into action under the circumstances:

Downsizing

Downsizing is a reduction in the workforce of an organization. Typically, this means the same amount of work is absorbed by fewer people. This change is often stressful for the remaining employees who are forced to pick up the slack, but this is not the case if there was not enough work for the personnel employed before the downsizing.

Downsizing is not the same as a layoff. Layoffs are often done temporarily with the intent of bringing employees back when business picks up. Downsizing is a more permanent action with the intent of never bringing back the employees who were let go.

Downsizing occurs for several reasons including:

- An organization is no longer profitable.
- An organization wants to increase profitability.
- An organization has experienced a reduction in sales or business volume.
- An organization is about to experience a reduction in sales or business volume.
- An organization is in financial trouble.
- An organization merges with another organization and positions overlap.

Regardless of the reason for downsizing, the result is a leaner workforce. Sometimes that workforce helps organizations survive while other times it is not enough to prevent organizations from shutting down.

OD in action

Downsizing helps surviving employees feel like they are valuable to their organizations because they were not let go. They were specifically chosen to move forward with their organizations, and this makes them feel important. Their employers have faith in them, and this makes them feel committed to helping their companies "rise from the ashes" and achieve greater goals. At this point, OD is not needed...but that soon changes.

After the initial relief of surviving a downsizing, employees begin to experience concern about their own job security. They are not sure what is going to happen next, and this causes distress. They need to decide if they are going to wait to see what happens or look for employment elsewhere. OD helps employees understand that they survived due to their value to their employers, and that value will remain.

OD also helps employees maintain confidence in their employers. Understandably, employees are not certain that their leadership can guide them out of the current mess and move them into a better situation. Their negative reactions to change threaten to impact the entire culture of their organizations, but OD combats this threat. Specifically, OD is implemented to explain the reasons for the downsizing. Workers are told why this difficult decision had to be made and what the short-term and long-term expectations are for the future.

OD also assures employees are involved during the entire downsizing process and after it is complete. It helps them understand their roles and counteract the lower morale that often results. This is done using honesty...even if that honesty is not all positive. Employees are going through a difficult period, and they want to be informed of important happenings in the organization. Traditional meetings are the best way to do this because employees have an opportunity to ask questions about their concerns, but surveys are a good way to tap the surviving employees' perceptions of the downsizing aftermath. The information can be used to improve the workplace environment by targeting the things that matter the most. Sometimes people are more honest in a survey than they are when talking directly to those in charge of the OD...if the survey is anonymous.

One common mistake that plant managers make after downsizing is failing to include supervisors in the discussions. Supervisors need to be included because they are also impacted by downsizings. They are looked at as representatives of the management team, but sometimes their understanding of what transpired is no more than that of the employees who work for them. Supervisors also need information so they can answer their employees' questions accurately.

Image revisions

Image is important for organizations because it shows how they are perceived by outsiders. For example, manufacturing companies are perceived ethically based on the ways they treat the environment, employees, suppliers, customers, and the public. They are expected to recycle, properly dispose of waste, be fair to their employees, and be truthful to customers about products or services. They are also expected not to play favorites due to friendships, family relationships, or romances. In short, this ethical responsibility involves refraining from behavior that is questionable even though it is not necessarily illegal...which means going above and beyond what is required by the law.

Image is also based on the perception of an organization's philanthropic actions. Companies are judged based on their promotion of charitable organizations by giving donations or providing services free of charge. Sometimes employees also get involved with charity by donating their time. Regardless of the method of giving, it reflects well on the perception of organizations because they are viewed as being charitable.

OD in action

Organizational development is about getting employees to embrace the necessary changes for goal accomplishment. In terms of image, OD helps organizations become more innovative by acting before problems occur. For example, an oil manufacturing company could contribute to charitable organizations that help wildlife after their habitat has been destroyed. This must be done before, not after, the company has its own oil spill to show that they have invented a way to reach out to the community without being in an emergency. This action will reflect well on the oil company if they make a mistake and damage the environment in the future. In short, organizations must be proactive instead of reactive to improve their image.

OD also helps organizations invest in ongoing efforts to maintain and improve their image. For example, a strategy can be put into effect that assures employees find job satisfaction. This prevents future ethical problems by addressing issues before they fester into something bigger. In short, a little time and money invested now can prevent a lot of time and money from being spent on improving a bad image later.

Astute plant managers hold themselves accountable for all organizational actions regardless of the nature of those actions. In terms of image, OD makes sure leaders have a vision and hold themselves accountable for making sure employees are working toward that vision. This requires delegation and monitoring to make sure tasks are getting completed. For example, a plant manager might have a vision of eliminating all unethical behavior of management personnel. A goal of zero tolerance for bribery from vendors is established, and it is monitored with quarterly audits designed to look for potential occurrences of any type of unethical payoff. In short, plant managers need to establish a vision of image and make sure employees are doing the things necessary to reach the goals related to that vision.

OD promotes listening, and plant managers need to listen to the things people are saying about their organizations to maintain a good image. Many times, this can only be done by asking questions because people do not always volunteer information. For example, a chemical company that generates unpleasant smells could analyze the environmental impact by listening to local residents. The information received could be used to develop systems that reduce the most offensive smells. Along the same lines, the company could also institute a community program that educates the local residents about these odors and their effects. These actions create an ongoing dialog with local folks, and they all stem from listening to the concerns of people.

Mergers and acquisitions

Mergers and acquisitions typically require organizational development more than any other aspect of business because all people associated are impacted...including customers, suppliers, employees, and other stakeholders. This impact makes OD essential for goals and objectives to be achieved.

Some companies have a goal of growth, so they develop a strategy to grow by acquiring other companies. They identify organizations that they think will help them obtain their objective, and then they begin the acquisition process. This acquisition strategy can be very successful and lead to fast growth. Companies can literally double in size overnight, thereby becoming more competitive and profitable. However, this strategy can also lead to financial problems, including bankruptcy, if cash flow is depleted or a purchased company turns out to be a loser.

Companies also buy competitors with the sole intent of eliminating them from the market. They do not want the competition, so they buy it and put an end to it. Leaders of organizations who choose to behave in this manner often fall under the watchful eye of the United States government because they might be violating antitrust laws....and an illegal monopoly could result.

The last reason companies merge with or acquire other companies is for diversity. Like people, businesses have different strengths. For example, one company is good at distributing products, while another is strong in customer service. Leadership from both companies respects each other, so they decide to join forces. When this happens, two companies from seemingly unrelated industries become one. This might initially seem strange to some outsiders, but it makes sense from a diversification standpoint. Leaders of organizations do not want all their eggs in one basket, so they seek to broaden their organization's standing by establishing roots in other areas. This action is similar to investors in the stock market who wants to diversify their portfolios. They do not want all their money in one sector, such as technology, because the market might tank in that sector. They feel safer investing in different sectors with the goal of slowly growing the entire portfolio over time. However, also like the stock market, there are risks involved with diversity that can lead to problems...such as lack of short-term funds or cash flow.

Diversity is important because employees from the companies merging together exchange thoughts and perspectives, and the differing viewpoints contribute to the overall effectiveness of the newly formed organization. This improves decision-making and allows goals to be achieved in designated time frames. For example, a company has strong manufacturing capabilities, but it lacks the marketing expertise to expand its product line. When they acquire a marketing company, they double their sales within a year due to the retail relationships the marketing company had in place before the acquisition. However, this process is not without problems because non-similarities of the two companies can be difficult to overcome.

OD in action

Organizational development works to motivate employees, and motivation inspires people to do their best. When motivation decreases, employees feel defeated and develop negative attitudes. Negative attitudes affect work performance because employees resort to doing the absolute minimum to get by. This is life-threatening for mergers and acquisitions because employees need to perform at higher levels than normal for the organization to reach goals and objectives.

Employees are capable of self-motivation in certain situations, but mergers and acquisitions present a unique set of circumstances that must be overcome. Workers need motivational help so their morale and attitudes do not deteriorate...and that help usually comes from organizational development. OD helps supervisors realize that motivation in these situations is very challenging because emotions are running high, and employees take the statements made to them very seriously. Plant managers who attempt to motivate employees by saying the wrong things often end up having the opposite effect and demotivating workers. This is especially true if the employees believe they are not being told the truth. False statements add insult to injury because workers are lied to in a situation that already makes them very uncomfortable.

OD also helps employees accept each other. Organizations operate differently, and people are used to working in certain ways. Add this to the fact that different customs and languages might now be the norm, especially if the merger or acquisition is global, and acceptance can become a major headache. Managers need to intervene to smooth out the problems that exist between employees. This might not be easy, but it is doable if an effort is made...and organizational development leads the way.

Organizational development helps employees, but it also helps ease the uncertainty experienced by plant managers because supervisors are often left in the dark during mergers and acquisitions. They are unsure of what is expected of them, and they are also unsure about what will happen in the future. OD supervisors understand their roles and provide accurate information to their employees.

Mergers and acquisitions create a new company, and many times that company needs to implement rules, regulations, policies, and procedures. For example, the formation of a large organization often requires a more bureaucratic structure. This does not always sit well with employees, but it is needed to communicate effectively and keep things fair and balanced. OD programs help to write policies and procedures, research the legal aspects of rule changes, and make sure regulations are doing what they are designed to do.

When two organizations unite as one, there are bound to be diversity issues. Age, gender, race, and religion all play roles here; and organizational development programs work to make sure people respect each other's differences and work together effectively. This is a serious issue because a lack of diversity can result in failure to accomplish goals...and it has the potential for lawsuits if people feel that they have experienced discrimination.

Mergers and acquisitions often result in changes in the new company's hierarchy. OD works to keep track of the changes and update the organizational chart. This might seem like a relatively simple task, but changes are fast and frequent after a merger or acquisition, and staying current sometimes presents a challenge.

Based on the above descriptions of organizational development in action, it is rather obvious that OD has some major benefits. The following are some of those benefits:

Improved personnel

The changes put in place by organizational development match employee skills to the demands of their workplace. As employees move into new roles, they develop skills that help them grow professionally and add value to their employers. The process of exposure, training, and application creates the mindset of continuous improvement that leads to the accomplishment of organizational goals and objectives.

Better bottom lines

Once the changes are in place and working, higher profitability results. Since profit is often the biggest indicator of organizational health and well-being, better bottom lines are considered the "crown jewel" of organizational development. When profits increase, employees have secure jobs and stockholders receive positive return-on-investment. Everyone is happy, and that happiness encourages the continuous improvement process.

Increased communication

Without a doubt, organizational development increases communication in organizations. This is partially due to the group concept that promotes input from everyone and requires all members to participate in decision-making processes. However, another reason for increased communication is the constant feedback that evolves from OD. Mandatory employee involvement leads to a wealth of feedback, and that feedback is incorporated into the continuous improvement cycle; thereby opening the floodgates for communication at all levels of the organization.

Higher standards

Organizational development raises the bar in many areas of workplaces. Processes and procedures are more efficient, and employees become committed to continuous improvement. These higher standards also produce better products and services that lead to new levels of customer satisfaction and organizational success.

Change is hard for many people to accept, and it is even more difficult for them to embrace. Organizational development facilitates change while emphasizing continuous improvement. Without OD, some companies are unable to change...and this prevents them from completing the tasks necessary to achieve goals and objectives.

Despite all the positives mentioned in this section, some negatives stem from organizational development. These negatives are discussed in the following section on disadvantages.

Employee resistance

This is the most common negative associated with organizational development. Regardless of how change is implemented, there are always some people who simply refuse to accept it. They do not want to stray from the old way of doing things because they have established a comfort zone that they do want to leave. These individuals must be left behind until they eventually accept the OD changes, find another job, or are terminated from the organization. Unfortunately, employee resistance is a harsh reality that sometimes needs to be dealt with using harsh actions.

Cost

As many plant managers of organizations have experienced, the payback for organizational development can be many times the investment.

However, that payback does not occur until the changes have been made and employees have been trained to perform in their new roles at optimum levels. This process has an initial cost associated with it, and some companies might find that cost too much to absorb. Consequently, these organizations choose to continue operating without any changes, and OD never gets off the ground.

Time

The changes involved with organizational development do not take place overnight. In fact, they sometimes take months or years to become the norm. The time required is sometimes too much for plant managers to swallow, and they end up putting OD programs on hold before they take root in the organization. When this happens, the changes that did take place do little or no good; thereby creating a negative perception of organizational development that is difficult to change.

Complexity

Although not necessarily designed to do so, organizational development tends to add to the structure of organizations. Job responsibilities are reassigned, groups are added, and processes and procedures are changed; all of which require planning and oversight. Planning and oversight are also needed for getting all employees involved with the changes taking place, and this is never a simple task. Worse yet, complexity slows productivity making it even more difficult to remain positive about the future of organizational development. The complexity of organizational development is not a major threat, but it can hinder companies that are used to operating in much simpler modes.

As you can clearly see, there are some disadvantages associated with organizational development. These negatives mean there is room for improvement. The suggestions for improving organizational development are simple and straightforward. However, these improvements tend to get overlooked because plant managers believe they know what is best for their organizations. If these leaders truly want their workplaces to become more efficient, then they need to incorporate the following improvements:

Understand true organizational goals and objectives

Some manufacturing companies that implement organizational development are not sure about what they are trying to accomplish. If this is the case, then OD will not be beneficial. In fact, it will likely be detrimental. Based on this, plant managers need to understand their goals and objectives before undergoing OD. This might mean conducting a study or assigning a task force to determine goals and objectives, but the time and effort invested are necessary and will not be wasted.

Understand the importance of involving employees at all levels

Plant managers sometimes fail to understand that organizational development requires participation by all employees...from the lowest members to the highest members of the hierarchy. These leaders put people in charge of OD and expect them to carry out every aspect of the program purely from a management perspective. Without the input of everyone, goals and objectives cannot be realized because problems at all levels do not surface. Quite simply, the changes being made do not address the core issues of the organization, and OD turns into a waste of money, time, and effort.

Understand the meaning of continuous improvement

Plant managers need to realize that organizational development means the bar is continually being raised. The "good enough" mentality needs to be replaced with the thinking that organizations can always get better. Unfortunately, it is a painful process to continually look for faults or areas in need of change. However, OD struggles to find success without a continuous improvement mindset, and that mindset starts at the top of the organization.

Understand the need for experts

Some organizations are simply not equipped to handle organizational development programs. They do not have the skills or resources to make it happen, so they implement it without fully understanding its potential. IF this is the case, then organizations are crippled right from the start...and things will only get worse. This problem can be avoided by reaching out to others for assistance. Reaching out can be expensive, but the money spent needs to be thought of as an investment that will be recouped over time. In short, plant managers need to consider using outside consultants or they jeopardize the benefits OD offers.

Risk management

Organizations experience a wide variety of risks, and plant managers need to make decisions based on the potential rewards or consequences of those risks. They do this by implementing programs known as risk management. These programs are designed to reduce uncertainty in organizations when the effects of something that might happen are unknown. This is important because negative effects can compromise the goals and objectives of organizations...and they can even lead to manufacturing facilities shutting down.

Uncertain times have led many manufacturers to stop forecasting or predicting their future. Economic downfalls, terrorism threats, environmental concerns, and political changes have all impacted the way business is conducted, and this has led to plant managers being more discrete about their short-term and long-term plans. Uncertainties have also resulted in plant managers focusing on risk management more than they have ever done in the past. They try to identify the most significant risks in their organizations and act accordingly with programs designed to reduce or eliminate them.

Essentially, any actions that reduce or eliminate risk fall under the umbrella of risk management. These actions help organizations secure their future by warding off potential problems before they occur. Risk management allows manufacturers to make business decisions with confidence, and it also provides options when potential problems become reality. Companies that make decisions without evaluating risk are gambling...and that gambling can lead to their demise.

Risk management programs also play a big role in protecting manufacturing facilities from potential catastrophes. These programs are put into place for decision-making that identifies potential danger and works toward preventing or eliminating it. In short, they help organizations achieve goals and objectives while controlling the risks involved.

There are two basic types of risk management of concern to plant managers. These types are quantitative and qualitative, and they are broken down as follows:

Quantitative

Quantitative risk management determines the cost of catastrophic situations by establishing the probability of occurrence and the potential consequences resulting from that occurrence. It classifies and evaluates the impact of problems on organizations and their employees. In short, it determines the cost of lost productivity, replacement of assets, and damaged reputation using statistical analysis. For example, the meat processing risk management team might use a continuous variable commonly known as return on investment (ROI) to determine the standard deviation (variance) of financial risk. First, they identify the threats that produce the biggest estimated losses, and then they determine appropriate measures to reduce those losses.

An advantage of quantitative risk management is the results are objective. Personal bias is not a factor because statistical analysis is used to determine risk. However, a disadvantage of quantitative risk management is the complexity of the process because the calculation of results can be difficult and cumbersome.

Qualitative

Qualitative risk management does not utilize statistical analysis and is therefore used by many small organizations. It uses relative values to determine potential loss if a problem occurs. In short, it awards scores for the probability of problematic situations and the need for action to minimize the risk involved. For example, if a company is located in Detroit (Michigan), then the risk management team might evaluate the probability of a hurricane as insignificant and the need to take action to reduce the risk as very minor. Along the same lines, they might evaluate the probability of employees missing work as very likely and the need to take action to reduce risk as major.

Advantages of qualitative risk management include ease of calculation and implementation. The method is relatively simple to understand and implement in most organizations.

However, a major disadvantage is personal bias. Lack of statistical analyses allows employees the ability to manipulate results based on their perceptions of situations.

Plant managers need to understand the six steps involved in a risk management program. All steps are listed below using a meat processing company as an example for each.

Assemble

This step involves assembling the risk management team. Care needs to be taken when selecting people because there should be a mixture of job responsibilities and personalities that allows the team to identify and analyze risk from multiple perspectives without bias. Work experience is also important because veteran employees typically have knowledge that is worth its weight in gold...and new employees often make suggestions that were previously never considered. The goal of the selection process is to make sure the team is heterogeneous so members do not all think the same. Diversity is the key to assessing risk in any situation.

Example

A meat processing company decides to implement a risk management program. They start by assembling a risk management team that consists of the plant manager, quality manager, sales manager, distribution manager, and office manager.

The plant manager and quality manager have been with the organization for more than 15 years. They have seen the company go through growth phases, and they also understand what they need to do when sales slow and times get tough. They have a very good grasp of the processes, policies, and procedures that are utilized for manufacturing meat products. In short, their experience is very valuable because they understand many of the risks involved when running a production facility.

The sales manager does not fully understand plant operations, but she is well aware of customer needs. She has only been with the company for six months, but prior to this job, she worked for a competitor for seven years. She sees risks involved with product being out in the field...particularly those that involve food safety because the last company she worked for had a product recall due to bacterial contamination. This experience causes her to perceive the risk of recall as very serious.

The distribution manager has been with the meat processing company for over three years. He understands finished product storage, inventory, and transportation. He perceives product loss, damage, and theft as the biggest risks in his department because he has the unfortunate experience of seeing all three of these problems occur while product is stored or transported to other locations. His finished product perception makes him a valuable member of the risk management team.

The office manager understands record storage, customer service, accounting, and payroll. She realizes embezzlement and other white-collar theft are potential issues. She also knows the risks involved with calculating employee hours worked, paying invoices, or collecting money owed to the company. She views risks from an administrative standpoint, and her perception adds diversity to the risk management team.

Identify

This is where risks are realized. Each team member identifies and documents the risks that they see in their organization. Their perception is valuable because everyone perceives things differently.

This procedure should not take place in meetings because (1) some team members are more dominant than others and (2) there is potential for groupthink. Each member needs to think independently and document the risks they determine to be important. This asynchronous process gives all members flexibility so they can fit their thinking into their routine work schedules.

Example

The risk management team members at the meat processing company think about risks from their perspectives and identify them as follows:

Plant manager

Risks identified: power, productivity, nature, inventory, staffing, attendance

More specifically:

- *Power* refers to the risk of power outages
- *Productivity* refers to the risk of losing manufacturing productivity
- *Nature* refers to the risk of natural disasters (tornados, high winds, lightning strikes, earthquakes, etc.)
- *Inventory* refers to the risk of overstocking or understocking raw materials
- *Staffing* refers to the risk of having the right people for the jobs
- *Attendance* refers to the risk of people not showing up for their jobs (due to strikes, sickness, vacations, etc.)

Quality manager

Risks identified: allergens, bacteria, metal, chemicals, flavor, appearance

More specifically:

- *Allergens* refer to the risk of exposing people to ingredients that give them allergic reactions
- *Bacteria* refers to the risk of product being contaminated with disease-causing bacteria
- *Metal* refers to the risk of product being contaminated with metal
- *Chemicals* refers to the risk of product being contaminated with chemicals

- *Flavor* refers to the risk of products having an off taste
- *Appearance* refers to the risk of color and shape being wrong

Sales manager

Risks identified: product recalls, price, new products, service, quality, availability

More specifically:

- *Product recalls* refers to the risk of product being recalled back to the company for consumer safety once it has been shipped
- *Price* refers to the risk of customers not buying product because it costs too much
- *New products* refer to the risk of the company not producing the new products necessary to compete
- *Service* refers to the risk of customers not being happy with the service provided to them
- *Quality* refers to the risk of product not meeting acceptable quality standards

Distribution manager

Risks identified: transportation, delivery vehicles, drivers, accidents, inventory, nature

More specifically:

- *Transpiration* refers to the risk of lost or damaged product during transportation
- *Delivery vehicles* refers to the risk of delivery vehicles not running properly when needed
- *Drivers* refers to the risk of driver shortages
- *Accidents* refers to the risk of drivers getting into accidents
- *Inventory* refers to the risk of inventory being inaccurate, stolen, or lost.
- *Nature* refers to the risk of bad weather that prevents delivery of products

Office manager

Risks identified: customer satisfaction, employee ethics, theft, attendance, payables, receivables

More specifically:

- *Customer satisfaction* refers to the risk of customers not being satisfied with products or service
- *Employee ethics* refers to the risk of unethical employee actions
- *Theft* refers to the risk of white-collar theft
- *Attendance* refers to the risk of employees missing excessive time at work
- *Payables* refers to the risk of suppliers not being paid
- *Receivables* refers to the risk of customers not paying their bills

Analyze

Now the team gets together to categorize the risks that have been submitted by individual members. Some risks overlap and can be combined in the same category, others need their own separate category, and still, others are eliminated. These categories define the type of risk and its potential impact on organizational goals and objectives. They also create a solid structure that helps facilitate the next step of the process (evaluate).

Example

The risk management team members at the meat processing company reduce the identified risks to the following categories:

Natural disasters

This includes inclement weather, tornadoes, earthquakes, lightning, flooding, snowdrifts, and flooding.

Food safety

This includes product recalls, product spoilage, and product contamination.

Customer satisfaction

This includes price, delivery, order fulfillment, and quality.

Employee attendance

This includes delivery personnel, production personnel, and replacement personnel.

Finances

This includes payables and receivables.

Employee ethics

This includes unethical and illegal employee actions.

Inventory

This includes shortages and overages of finished product or raw materials

Evaluate

After risks have been categorized, it is time to rank them in order of importance. Typically this is done by evaluating each risk for its potential to occur and consequences that can result. Some risks are important enough to be quickly addressed in the next step while others can be moved to the backburner.

This step is sometimes considered the most difficult because inaccurate evaluations can lead to unanticipated problems...essentially defeating the purpose of the risk management team. However, there is a need for an order of importance, and evaluation addresses that need.

Example

The risk management team members at the meat processing company establish the following order of importance:

Employee attendance

Why? Employee attendance is a threat virtually every day. It is hard to get everyone to show up for work, and productivity is hindered on a fairly regular basis. For this reason, employee attendance ranks first on the list of important risks.

Food safety

Why? The meat processing company has not had a recall, and they have only had one complaint of a customer getting sick. However, the potential is there and the consequences could be devastating. Allergens are also present in the plant, and there is a risk that they could contaminate products without being listed in the ingredient statements.

Customer satisfaction

Why? Sales are critical for the meat processing company. A large reduction in sales volume could risk the survival of the organization.

Finances

Why? Vendors must be paid for their services or they will discontinue being vendors, and the meat processing company must get paid to have money to operate. Based on this, financial risk potentially threatens the well-being of the organization.

Inventory

Why? Raw material and finished product inventory outages affect the fulfillment of customer orders, and inventory overages tie up money that could be used elsewhere. This is a risk with inventory, but it is not major.

Natural disasters

Why? Tornadoes and flooding are threats that can occur with little or no warning. These weather disasters are a longshot, but they do present a minimum risk.

Employee ethics

Why? Unethical and illegal concerns have not been a problem in the past, but the potential for their occurrence does exist on a small level. For this reason, employee ethics receive the lowest ranking in terms of risk importance.

Address

Once risks have been categorized and ranked, it is time to address those that have been determined to be the most important. This is commonly referred to as response planning, and it is where the treatment begins. This treatment involves reducing the risks to acceptable levels using strategic planning and contingency planning. The goal is to minimize the probability of negative risks (strategic planning) while determining ways to address the problems that result when risks become reality (contingency planning).

Unfortunately, contingency planning often faces two major obstacles. These obstacles are:

Motivation

Contingency planning is essentially a backup plan that goes into effect if the strategic plan is not successful. Many risk management teams put so much time and effort into their strategic plan that they think it will be successful regardless of the circumstances. They simply believe that they will not need a contingency plan, so they are not motivated to create one.

Urgency

In reality, there is a low probability of a situation that will require a contingency plan. Yes, some circumstances create a crisis, but those circumstances are viewed as few and far between....so contingency planning moves to the bottom of the list in terms of importance. When something is a low-importance priority, it tends to never get done properly because there is no sense of urgency.

Example

The risk management team members at the meat processing company establish the following risk reduction measures as part of their strategic plan:

Employee attendance

On the job training is conducted at the plant, and this reduces the risk of employees missing work due to injuries. Job rotation is also ongoing; thereby allowing employees to learn each other's jobs and function as backups.

Food safety

A HACCP program is in place to address food safety in the plant. It pinpoints critical areas of meat processing to assure meat is safe when it leaves the plant. Additionally, all employees are educated on food safety and food defense. They are trained when they start with the meat processing company and on an annual basis.

Customer satisfaction

Surveys are sent to customers to assess their satisfaction. These surveys allow respondents to provide detailed information about why they are not happy.

Finances

All accounting and office personnel undergo initial and annual financial training specifically geared toward the meat processing company. This assures fewer mistakes will be made in the office.

Inventory

Employees conduct month-end inventory to reduce the risk of error, and weekly meetings are held between manufacturing, distribution, and purchasing personnel to discuss shortages and overages.

Natural disasters

The plant roof is inspected annually for damage, and the plant walls are constructed to withstand 70 MPH winds. This assures building security under severe weather conditions.

Employee ethics

A written ethics policy is given to all employees when they are hired. They must (1) pass a written test that shows they understand the policy and (2) sign off that they are in possession of the policy.

As part of their contingency plant, the risk management team members at the meat processing company establish the following to reduce problems that occur when risks become reality:

Employee attendance

A contract is established with a temporary staffing firm if the company experiences employee shortages. This firm can provide up to 100 employees within one hour of being contacted by the meat processing company.

Food safety

Mock recalls are conducted to assure all affected product can be recalled. These recalls trace all raw materials to original sources and all finished products to end-users. A law firm has also been contracted to handle interaction with the government and others if a recall becomes public.

Customer satisfaction

A policy is in place that refunds customers the product purchase price if they are not satisfied with it for any reason. Customers merely need to show proof of purchase, and they will be promptly refunded.

Finances

Internal audits are performed for all major financial discrepancies, and a contracted CPA firm is available for consultation.

Inventory

Internal investigations are performed for all major inventory discrepancies, and a contracted CPA firm is available for consultation.

Natural disasters

Local authorities (police, fire, utilities) are contacted to assess the situation and recommend a course of action. These individuals are trained in natural disaster response, and they have access to resources that are not available to the meat processing company.

Employee ethics

Internal investigations are performed for all unethical or illegal activities, and a contracted law firm is available for consultation.

Monitor

At this point, the risk management team has identified, analyzed, evaluated, and addressed important risks in their organization. However, the program still needs to be monitored to assure that it is working properly.

In this step, questions need to be asked. Is the program working as intended? Are the established controls still effective? Will the established controls be effective in the future? What are the weak points? What needs to be changed? If the program has been successful, then it can be left as is without change. However, if the program has failed or the future points towards its failure, then changes need to be made.

Example

The risk management team members at the meat processing company monitor the program as follows:

Employee attendance

Employee attendance is monitored using an employee attendance system that has a two-fold effect. It rewards employees with good attendance and disciplines those with poor attendance. Additionally, the fill-rate of the temporary employer is tracked. If the fill-rate falls below 80 percent, then other temporary employment services are explored as an option.

Food safety

Trends are tracked for all food safety deviations from the HACCP plan. Established trends require the meat processing company to make changes to processes and procedures to prevent future reoccurrences.

Customer satisfaction

Data from customer surveys is collected and analyzed for trends. Any negative trends require changes to be made to prevent reoccurrences.

Finances

All accounts payable and accounts receivable errors are documented. If a trend develops, then action is taken to determine why that trend occurred and how it can be prevented from reoccurring.

Inventory

Inventory outages and overages are tracked and documented. If a trend develops, then meetings are held to determine why the problem occurred and how to prevent a reoccurrence.

Natural disasters

All damage is documented on a list. Management reviews the list to find weak points that can be made stronger to prevent a recurrence.

Employee ethics

Unethical employee behavior is documented and disciplinary action is taken to prevent a reoccurrence. This discipline can involve employee termination and/or legal action.

The above steps outline a risk management program in a manufacturing facility. Plant managers do not necessarily have to oversee every step involved, but they need to understand the overall process to minimize the risks involved in running a successful operation.

Audits

Auditing is the process of reviewing records, documents, and processes of organizations to assure that those organizations are doing what they are supposed to be doing and providing accurate information. In many ways, audits function as risk analyses that hold management accountable for problems that have already occurred or could potentially occur. Since plant managers are at the top of the management chart in manufacturing facilities, they must understand the auditing of their operations.

Audits can be performed by internal personnel, but they are typically the most effective when they are conducted by external individuals (commonly known as a third party) who are unbiased and have some type of expertise in the subject matter. Internal and external audits are described below.

Internal

These audits are conducted by people who work for the companies that they are auditing. They might appear to be of little value due to the bias involved, but they are actually very beneficial when done correctly. Organizations change when processes are not working as designed, and this improves operations and helps plant managers accomplish goals and objectives.

Internal auditors look for record deviations and deficiencies using pre-determined qualitative analyses (such as interviews with employees) and quantitative analyses (such as a physical count of inventory). Performance scores are issued based on expectations and findings are often used to develop standards that are put in place to help organizations measure people and processes. In manufacturing facilities, many important plant management decisions are made based on these measurements.

In short, internal audits identify fraudulent activities, unethical behavior, unnecessary risks, and ineffective management. When confronted with these problems, plant managers of organizations must react or their organizations could fail to compete in their respective markets. If audit findings are completely ignored, then organizations risk the possibility of ceasing to exist.

External

External auditors perform many of the same functions as internal auditors, and they are subject to the same code of ethics and conduct. However, unlike internal audits, external audits are conducted by independent third-party professionals to assure the elimination of bias. External audits also extend beyond the scope of internal audits because they are more interested in the needs of customers and the rules put in place by regulatory agencies.

External auditors are usually highly qualified because they have gone through some type of training or certification process specific to the job, department, company, or industry that they are auditing. They provide a good snapshot of what is actually happening in the workplaces of their clients, and this provides generalizations that can be made about those workplaces and the people in them.

In short, external audits identify areas where organizations fall short of established requirements and standards. Auditors are independent of the organization being audited, and they are knowledgeable in the subject areas that they monitor; thereby adding a dimension to the auditing process that cannot be achieved by employees auditing their own organizations.

As most plant managers have experienced, audits are now ordinary occurrences in manufacturing facilities, and the demand for them is continuously growing. Many people associate audits with the financial aspects of organizations. They are correct because finances are often involved, but just about any subject matter can be audited as long as standards or benchmarks are available for measurement. For example, ethical audits are becoming quite popular today. These audits focus on the treatment of employees working at organizations, but they also move down the supply chain and investigate the treatment of the employees that work for the suppliers of those organizations. They want to make sure factors such as unpaid or forced labor are not involved at any level.

However, regardless of the subject matter involved, auditors use systematic procedures to assure organizations are meeting established protocols.

A comprehensive list of every type of audit is far too extensive for the scope of this book, but some of the most common types that plant managers experience are listed below.

Operations

This type of audit examines an entire organization for efficiency and effectiveness. Essentially, it is a detailed and comprehensive audit to assure that organizational objectives are being achieved. If those objectives are not being achieved, then changes must be implemented for compliance purposes.

Operational audits review organizational activities by focusing on efficiency, economy, and effectiveness. Auditors gather information on resources, time, and money so they can establish patterns, identify weak points, and point out areas that require improvement. The data used to make decisions for improvement typically comes from operational policies and the success or failure of those policies.

This type of audit can be simple, such as analyzing one group, or complex, such as analyzing an entire global organization. However, regardless of the complexity, an operations audit offers new ideas and concepts for future risk management.

An example of a task performed by an auditor during an operations audit is to focus on one dimension of organizational performance. Performance dimensions include cost, quality, effectiveness, efficiency, work environment, and value, and the auditor chooses to look at the effectiveness of policy development. He asks questions regarding the process that management uses to change policies including people involved, resources utilized, risks analyzed, documents generated, and time required. The goal is to find out if the policy development process truly is effective.

Quality

Quality audits can be administered in just about any area of business. They are essential for verifying whether or not organizations conform to established standards. They examine processes, products, and procedures and judge effectiveness and efficiency from a quality standpoint. They also indicate the ability of organizations to reduce problems and eliminate negative trends; thereby making them a great management tool for constructive criticism and self-improvement.

The global marketplace today is based on speed, quality, and convenience more now than it has ever been in the past. Customers demand quality and want to be sure the products and services they are purchasing meet the standards they are supposed to meet. The best way to gain that confidence is through a quality audit. Like other audits, the goal of quality audits is to point out non-conformances and push organizations toward continuous improvement. However, unlike some other audits, quality audits also point out areas where organizations are meeting or exceeding expectations. In short, these audits point out the good and bad aspects of quality in organizations...and some people find this very beneficial when always striving to improve.

An example of a task performed by an auditor during a quality audit of a manufacturing plant is making sure preventative maintenance is in place to prevent production machinery from breaking. The auditor asks for written procedures and logs with signatures of the people who have completed the designated maintenance tasks. Lack of this documentation signifies a lapse in the process and requires the job shop to make improvements before they are allowed to pass the audit.

Financial

This is probably the most well-known type of audit simply because most people associate auditing with finances. There are many government rules regarding finance in organizations, and a major part of a financial audit is to decide if standards for those rules are met or exceeded. Some organizations purposefully violate rules related to accounting to change their appearance on paper, while other organizations make honest mistakes that lead to incorrect documentation. However, regardless of the intent, financial audits are designed to expose monetary discrepancies so the reality of an organization's financial standing is accurately portrayed on paper.

Financial audits are important because false financial information deceives investors, lending institutions, government agencies, customers, suppliers, and employees. For example, an investment group might partner up with a company because that company is positioned in a market that appears to be ready to "explode" in terms of growth. This company is one of a select few that is profitable now, and the future looks much brighter than it does for those who currently are operating at a loss. However, if that company is falsifying documents to show a profit rather than a loss, then the investors are being deceived. Along the same lines, employees who work for the same company might look elsewhere for employment if they knew the reality of that company's finances.

A financial audit is best explained by listing the more common actions of auditors during the overall process. These actions include:

Confirmation

Numbers need to be verified, and that verification is only possible when auditors do the counting by themselves. Auditors cannot rely on counting by staff in the organization being audited because they need to assure that the numbers match the numbers on paper. In other words, auditors need confirmation that the organization being audited is presenting accurate information.

An example of confirmation during a manufacturing plant financial audit is an auditor who needs to verify the physical inventory of finished products. She goes into the finished product storage area and counts the number of products on hand, and then verifies the legitimacy of that number by matching it to the record given to her by the organization being audited. If the numbers do not match, then there is a problem in the inventory process.

Inquiry

Essentially, inquiry involves asking questions. Typical inquiry questions related to an examination of a monetary process during a financial audit include:

- Does this monetary process adhere to written procedures?
- How often does this monetary process take place?
- Where does this money from this monetary process end up?
- Who assures the success or failure of this monetary process?
- What happens if this monetary process fails?

The number of questions asked varies based on the importance of the information, focus of the audit, and style of the auditor, but the point is that inquiry is a major action taken by auditors because, without inquiry, there is no audit.

An example of an inquiry during a financial audit is an auditor who is reviewing the entire process of a manufacturer's 401K retirement plan. He sees that pay is being deducted from employees' paychecks weekly and transferred to individual employee accounts in an investment company that offers mutual funds, money markets, government securities, and bonds as investment options. However, he does not see who is responsible for these transactions and what happens if the process does not work as expected, so he asks for a written plan. The plan shows that the CFO holds fiduciary responsibility for the accuracy and legitimacy of the plan, and government checks are in place to monitor her actions. If the retirement process does not work as expected, then the CEO and CFO are held accountable.

Observation

A lot of information can be gathered by simply observing what is happening in an organization. The observation process does not involve asking questions, but it is designed to find answers.

Sometimes silent observations make employees nervous and they do things that they normally would not have done. However, after a little time, workers begin to forget about the auditor watching them and revert back to their normal ways of performing job tasks.

The amount of time auditors spend observing financial operations is based on findings. If suspect practices are noticed, then more time is spent watching people do their jobs. Along the same lines, a workplace that appears to be doing things "by the book" will likely have less scrutiny.

An example of observation during a financial audit is an auditor who is watching cashiers take in money at the retail outlet of a manufacturing facility. The cashiers must follow established standards to assure all money transactions, especially those involving cash, are accounted for so government taxes will be properly paid. If discrepancies are noticed, then they are documented and corrective action by the retailer is required.

Inspection

Virtually every organization generates records. These records document internal and external business transactions and they are useful when issues arise about something that happened in the past.

Unfortunately, the information on records is not always accurate, and inaccuracies are what auditors try to find. They inspect records to verify they are accurate, complete, and conform to established rules and regulations.

The number and/or severity of discrepancies dictate the amount of time auditors devote to the inspection of records. If records only have a few inaccuracies, then they might be overlooked to move on to more important matters. However, if there are multiple errors and/or evidence of falsification or fabrication, then auditors might choose to investigate further...and non-conformances will surely result.

An example of inspection during a financial audit is an auditor who peruses a financial statement to make sure generally accepted accounting principles (commonly referred to as GAAP) are being used and followed. These principles meet the requirements of the Security and Exchange Commission, and deviation from them is a warning sign that mistakes are being made, information is being withheld, and/or documents are being falsified.

Tracing

Tracing is similar to tracking because both have the goal of finding something. However, tracing differs from tracking because it usually starts at the end of the process rather than the beginning. It looks at the end result and tries to determine what it is made up of and how it got there.

Typically, tracing during an audit is limited to one or two processes due to time constraints. Auditors have a limited amount of time that they can spend on this activity because other important matters also need to be examined. One or two tracing exercises fall well short of a complete analysis, but the processes monitored provides a snapshot of what is happening in the organization.

An example of tracing during a financial audit is an auditor who starts with money in the bank account of a manufacturing plant and works backward to find the original source of that money. She looks for a paper trail of transactions to verify that everything was done following government rules and regulations. If any step of the process cannot be uncovered, then discrepancies exist that could lead to non-compliances.

Safety

Safety audits are important because the risks they identify can save people's lives, while other audits are not capable of doing the same. The auditor often works with the Occupational Safety and Health Administration (commonly known as OSHA), a government agency that focuses on people's health and safety in workplaces. Machines, jobs, processes, and people are monitored by auditors, and non-conformances are issued for deviations from rules and regulations. In a nutshell, the goal of a safety audit is to pinpoint areas where safety risks can be minimized or eliminated; thereby protecting employees from physical injury and giving them peace of mind that they can perform their jobs without the fear of getting hurt.

A typical safety auditor examines an organization's written health and safety program and decides if management is committed to that program. This commitment includes supplying the proper resources (usually time and money) for the program, assigning job responsibilities to those in charge of the program, determining the success or failure of the program, and making changes to improve the program.

An example of a task performed by an auditor during a safety audit is an interview with manufacturing employees to see if they are comfortable operating machinery and doing their jobs. These employees are asked questions related to their health, safety, and general well-being in the workplace. The auditor can then determine if workers feel that they can express safety concerns to management without the fear of retaliation. These interviews are also used to determine management commitment in terms of providing the proper resources (such as money for personal protective equipment, machine guards, safeties, etc.)

Ethics

This type of audit is saved for last because of its recent growth in popularity (as noted in the introduction of this book). More and more companies, especially those that are large, are requiring their suppliers to undergo ethics audits to assure the employees of those suppliers are treated properly. These audits examine employees' pay, benefits, hours worked, and working conditions. If abuse is discovered, then the supplier must take corrective action or risk losing the business.

Interestingly, ethics audits also go farther down the supply chain to examine the companies that sell goods and services to the suppliers being audited. If the goods or services come from companies that are known to violate human rights, then the suppliers will not be allowed to buy from them. Suppliers that refuse to abide by the ethics guidelines are removed as approved vendors.

In short, ethics audits are put in place to protect workers (often production workers). This protection is important to companies that are known worldwide, such as Wal-Mart, because they have public images to protect. Leaders of these companies understand that poor images lead to damaged reputations and boycotts of products and services...which can be very financially damaging.

An example of a task performed by an auditor during an ethics audit is a check on the rate of pay for hourly production employees who are working overtime along with the number of overtime hours those employees are required to work.

Overtime hourly pay must be at least 1.5 times the amount paid for regular hours worked or regulations are violated. Additionally, some rules limit the number of hours worked in one day to twelve, so overtime can only be mandatory for four hours after the regular shift ends.

There are many other types of audits in addition to those listed above, but discussing every one of these is not possible in the scope of this book. However, the audits that are discussed that show why they are important for plant managers to understand.

Social responsibility

The last section discusses social responsibility. Essentially, social responsibility is an obligation to behave in ways that positively impact society. For plant managers, this means that profit is not their only concern. In fact, in some cases, profitability can take a backseat to assuring nothing harmful is done to society.

Some plant managers find it difficult to put any aspect of business on the same level as financial success. After all, money drives manufacturing facilities because, without it, those facilities would cease to exist. However, it has been suggested that social responsibility leads to profitability because many socially responsible thoughts and ideas are generated by the public...and manufacturers that ignore those thoughts and ideas have difficulty selling their products.

Businesses become socially responsible in one of two ways. The first way involves internal actions that make sure the organization or the people in it do not engage in any type of socially harmful actions. An example is a foundry that invites the EPA to inspect the soil on their property for contamination that might harm the environment. This inspection is not required, but it goes "above and beyond" to protect the environment. The second way involves external actions that do something to directly advance socially responsible goals and objectives. An example is a chemical plant that invests money and time into planting trees in urban areas. They did not do any damage to the areas that working toward beautifying, but they want to show that they are concerned about the environment and take appropriate action to highlight that concern.

Social responsibility for businesses came into the spotlight a few decades ago and it has continued to attract attention and grow in popularity. In the early 1990s, Archie Carroll developed a socially responsible pyramid that defined four basic corporate responsibilities. This pyramid has basic stakeholder responsibilities at the bottom (legal and economic) and higher societal responsibilities (ethical and philanthropic) at the top. Similar to Abraham Maslow's Hierarchy of Needs, lower-level responsibilities of organizations must be met before moving on to the responsibilities that benefit society.

For this book, the social responsibilities of Carroll's pyramid are listed separately without regard to the importance of progression. An additional responsibility that addresses volunteering has also been added for better understanding. That being said, social responsibilities are as follows:

Economic

This is probably the most well-known type of social responsibility, and it refers to an organization's responsibilities to its stakeholders. Businesses are obligated to create jobs, offer valuable products and services, and provide a return-on-investment to stockholders and investors. Organizations must also operate as effectively and efficiently as possible while offering innovative products and services. Most business leaders understand this type of social responsibility and make it one of their top priorities because it helps grow their organizations and sustain their livelihoods.

An example of economic social responsibility is a bakery that enters the high-end market of organic bread. They know organic items are very trendy and profitable, and selling them will positively impact their bottom line. This keeps the company healthy and makes shareholders happy.

Ethical

This type of social responsibility is growing in importance. Companies are held accountable for the ways they treat the environment, employees, suppliers, customers, and the general public. They are expected to recycle, properly dispose of waste, be fair to their employees, and be truthful to customers about products or services. They are also expected not to play favorites due to friendships, family relationships, or romances. In short, this responsibility involves refraining from behavior that is questionable even though it is not necessarily illegal and acting responsibly in all situations. Sometimes this means going above and beyond what is required by the law.

An example of ethical social responsibility is a stamping plant that offers paid maternity leave to men and women. This is not required by law, but it is an ethical action that allows parents to spend time with new babies without worrying about finances. This shows that the company respects its employees and is concerned about their happiness and well-being.

Legal

Legal social responsibilities cannot be ignored because they are required by law. Organizations need to obey all laws established by the government. Government agencies that enforce laws include the Internal Revenue Service (IRS), Occupational Safety and Health Administration (OSHA), National Labor Relations Board (NLRB), and the Securities and Exchange Commission (SEC).

An example of legal social responsibility is a window manufacturer that keeps accurate track of all cash sales as required by law. Cash transactions can be difficult for the IRS to verify, so the window company makes sure these sales are transparent to avoid scrutiny or an audit. They make sure they adhere to the law by doing the right thing.

Philanthropic

This type of social responsibility involves promoting causes that organizations believe are justifiable. It is typically done by giving money in the form of donations, but it can also be in the form of services. Either way, the giving reflects well on the perception of organizations because they are viewed as being charitable.

An example of philanthropic social responsibility is an automotive supplier matching 100 percent of employee monetary donations to the St. Jude Children's Hospital. This action shows compassion and is for a good cause. It also encourages employees to donate by making them feel that their donations are important.

Volunteer

Volunteer social responsibilities do not involve the direct giving of money. Instead, employees offer their services for something that their employer believes is justifiable. This reflects well on the perception of organizations, and it gets people personally involved in a good cause.

An example of volunteer social responsibility is a pharmaceutical manufacturing company that recruits its employees to work at local soup kitchens. This action shows compassion for those who are less fortunate and it benefits the community. It also benefits the employees because they feel like they are doing something good for the community.

Social responsibility requires a big monetary commitment from manufacturing companies, and that commitment presents challenges...especially when profits are low. However, the impact on these organizations is far more than financial. It affects employees, customers, suppliers, and the public in positive and negative ways depending on perception as shown below.

Customers

This refers to the retention of current customers and the acquisitions of new ones. Some people simply will not buy products or services from organizations that they do not believe are socially responsible. Instead, they patronize businesses that share similar values.

This type of impact can have a "trickle-down" effect that goes quite deep. For example, a person might refuse to eat at a restaurant because the chicken that the restaurant sells comes from a farm that raises birds in cages rather than letting them live "free-range" style. This action directly impacts the restaurant, but it also indirectly affects the distributor that delivers the chicken, the processor that prepares the chicken, the slaughterhouse that kills the chicken, and the farmer that raises the chicken. In this case, the impact of the person's action is much deeper than it might appear on the surface.

Investment

Investors are needed by many companies, and social responsibility affects those investors. This effect can be positive or negative, depending on perception. For example, an investor might be looking for a company to put money into that is concerned about the environment. They will not invest in a business that is socially irresponsible in terms of the ecosystem....regardless of the potential for return-on-investment.

Like it or not, entire communities are sometimes affected by investment decisions. Small towns rely on businesses to support their economies because those businesses create jobs and generate tax revenue. If a company falls short of receiving an investment due to its inability to be socially responsible, then it can damage the financial well-being of many people who have nothing in common with that company other than to live in the same community.

Image

Every marketing professor knows the importance of image. In their minds, image makes or breaks organizations. Undoubtedly, social responsibility affects the image of companies all over the world. For example, "sweatshop manufacturers" in other nations that employ people at very low wages are frowned upon by people who are concerned about human rights and violations of ethical social responsibility. Along the same lines, an embezzlement scandal makes a financial institution look bad due to a disregard for economic social responsibility. In short, social responsibility forms images of organizations in people's minds...and a negative image can be very difficult to change.

An example of a negative image is a pharmaceutical manufacturer that keeps prices high on drugs that people need to survive so shareholders can profit immensely. This company has little concern for the individuals who need their medication, and the public perceives it as having an image of being uncaring and greedy. This image will be hard to change even if the company takes steps to replace economic social responsibility with ethical social responsibility.

Recruitment

As noted above, social responsibility is directly related to image. That image is ingrained in people's minds, and it is hard to alter. That image also drives the recruitment process because organizations with positive images are attractive to some potential employees. For example, younger employees often place high importance on the ecosystem. They prefer to work for organizations that are environmentally and socially responsible, and they will not consider employment with companies that have little regard for the environment.

Recruitment is influenced by the social responsibility of organizations more than many people realize. This is because some people's thinking is subliminal based on the values they have had in place since childhood. They instinctively react to situations based on their values, and this will not change unless their self-awareness is modified by some type of external stimuli or source.

Astute plant managers understand the potentially negative impact of social responsibility if they choose to ignore it, but this is not the only reason they have for embracing it. Social responsibility provides several other benefits for organizations. This should not come as a surprise, but most people do not realize these benefits because they associate social responsibility with increased costs. Sometimes this is true, but certain companies become more profitable by being socially responsible because the changes they undergo project a more positive image to stakeholders and the public.

In terms of leadership, the major advantages of social responsibility are as follows:

Reputation

There is an old saying that reputation follows people wherever they go. This saying is also true for organizations...but it needs to be expanded upon because, after a while, reputation progresses from a following to a leading role. It leads some companies to growth and prosperity, while it leads others to their graves.

Social responsibility establishes reputations because people see and hear things that influence their thinking. If they see a company donate to charity regularly, then they think highly of that organization. On the other hand, if they see a company where greed drives executives at the expense of others, then they think negatively about that organization.

In short, reputation is an important part of the perception that is driven by social responsibility. Plant managers that realize this importance find their organizations' socially responsible actions advantageous because they are viewed in a positive light by others.

Customer relationships

Socially responsible leaders build good relationships internally and externally. They establish a rapport with the charities they support, understand the needs of their stakeholders, and work well with the government agencies that regulate their actions. These relationships help build trust with customers because those customers understand the organizations they purchase suppliers and services from are legally, ethically, and economically responsible. Trust leads to the loyalty necessary for repeat business, and it prevents customers from looking for new companies to buy from just because they are less expensive. In short, social responsibility is advantageous because it helps establish and maintain solid customer relationships.

Compliance

Legal social responsibility is great for keeping organizations in compliance with rules and regulations. This is critical because violations cost money, and they can completely stop companies from operating. When manufacturers are compliant, their efficiency also improves so leaders can focus on doing their jobs rather than dealing with enforcement officers or auditors.

Compliance also reduces worry because there is no concern that regulatory actions could be around the corner. This is a significant benefit because worry leads to stress...and stress causes employees to burn out. In the long run, morale is increased, turnover is reduced, and the knowledge employees have acquired remains with their organizations.

Innovation

Innovation is necessary for the growth and prosperity of organizations. This innovation does not necessarily have to be cutting edge, but it needs to be present in some form. Innovation takes companies to the next level using new concepts and ideas, and it tends to snowball once it begins.

Astute plant managers realize that social responsibility helps people in their organizations become more innovative. It does this by forcing people to move outside of their comfort zones and still meet goals....often in ways that were never previously considered. For example, in the 1970s, the government forced automobile manufacturers to meet new fuel economy standards. Engineers started working on reducing the weight of cars so they would require less gas to operate. This led to the development of stronger, lighter, and more flexible materials that helped meet the new standards. However, an added plus was that these materials were also cheaper, which lead to a cost-saving that was previously unrealized.

One problem associated with social responsibility is that cost can get out of hand if it is not monitored closely by leaders. Programs designed to reduce environmental destruction through ethical practices or prevent disease through philanthropic actions can be expensive with no real way to recoup the money spent. This can cause manufacturing companies a variety of different problems including the inability to meet financial obligations.

This type of problem can have a huge impact on manufacturers with limited financial resources. They need money in more important areas of their businesses so they can continue to operate, even though their customers and the public might believe otherwise.

Another problem expands on the cost issue, and it might be the most common negative associated with social responsibility. Leaders of organizations have a fiduciary obligation to watch out for the best interests of stockholders, and that obligation is sometimes tossed aside in favor of social responsibility. Stockholders usually buy stock in a company because they want to earn income from the money they have invested. They want a return-on-investment (ROI), and that ROI is hindered by social responsibility because it does not produce income...at least in the short-term. In fact, some types of social responsibility, such as charitable donations, never generate income that can be readily seen. There are tax deductions for these types of financial transactions, but their impact on the bottom line is typically not good.

Not surprisingly, stockholders are often the most vocal opponents of social responsibility. They do not like seeing money come out of their pockets and put into something that might or might not be beneficial. Unfortunately, this issue will likely never go away as long as organizations continue to spend money on socially responsible actions.

Despite the problems involved, plant managers are more and more realizing the importance of social responsibility. They know that they must become more proactive in terms of being socially responsible and this involves innovation and investment. In terms of innovation, they must come up with ways to get better instead of waiting to be told what they need to do. In short, organizations must be proactive instead of reactive to improve their social responsibility.

In terms of investment, plant managers need to allocate resources for an ongoing effort to maintain and improve social responsibility. For example, employees can be designated to develop strategies and designate funding for projects that make sure workers find job satisfaction. This falls under ethical social responsibility, and it prevents future problems by addressing issues before they fester into something bigger. In short, a little time and money spent now can prevent a lot of time and money from being spent later on.

Plant managers need to spend time, money, and effort to move social responsibility forward in their organizations. This might present some challenges in the beginning, but the end results are worth the sacrifice.

Summary

Plant managers are often the most important employees in manufacturing facilities. They are in charge of all aspects of plant operations, and they interact with virtually everyone involved in the business. This book examines these unique individuals by analyzing what they do and how they function while describing the challenges they must overcome to perform at peak levels. It also highlights the many different skills that these leaders must possess to accomplish organizational goals and objectives.

This book has seven major areas of discussion including manufacturing, management, human resource management, organizational development, risk management, audits, and social responsibility. All of these areas are described and supported with examples to highlight their relationship to plant management. The reader is left with a broad analysis of the roles and responsibilities of the most essential leaders in manufacturing facilities, better known as plant managers.

Congratulations! You now understand more about plant management....an essential aspect of every manufacturing facility.